WRITING YOUR THESIS OR DISSERTATION

THE STUFF THEY MAY NOT TELL YOU

MORRIE MULLINS

Cover designed by Getcovers

ISBN (print): 979-8-9929152-0-4

ISBN (digital): 979-8-9929152-1-1

For Dad: My first and best editor, writing teacher, and friend. I miss you, and hope this does you proud.

FOREWORD

There are a lot of books about how to write a thesis or dissertation. Those books tell you, sometimes in generalities and sometimes in highly specific, very technical language, how to move from conceptualization of a thesis through its actualization. They offer practical advice and wisdom about this milestone in your academic and professional life, because (let's be honest...) we all need advice and assistance when approaching something we've not done before. What those books have in common is that they are sincerely trying to ease your process and help you succeed.

They are also, to varying degrees, full of crap. That full-of-crapness is not a malicious thing, nor is it about trying to separate you from your hard-earned money. (Not that you have a lot of that. You're in grad school.) It's well-intentioned full-of-crapness, birthed from the idea that a written text can teach someone how to create a more complex piece of written text. The difference between this book and others? Well, there are probably several.

When it comes to being full of crap, the difference is that I'm admitting it.

When it comes to substance, though, this book is not (just) about how to write. It's designed to help you refine how you *think about* writing your thesis/dissertation, offering you ways to step back and consider the process as you work through the conceptualization, execution, and completion of your document. And I'd really like the advice to continue to be helpful long after grad school is done.

A little about me, then. I'm an "expert" in a specific field: industrial-organizational (I-O) psychology. A big part of my job—and a part that I love—is teaching writing. I've mentored graduate students for twenty-plus years. I've chaired over eighty theses and dissertations (mainly theses; I taught, for most of my career, in a Master's program), and have sat on more thesis and dissertation committees than I can track. I have observed graduate student writing, as well as the graduate student experience of approaching, working through, and completing the thesis and dissertation, in graphic, bloody, joyous detail. I have read thousands of articles, reviewed for a number of journals, and served as editor for a professional publication. On top of that, for over twenty-five years there was only one day when I went to bed without having written at least 1,000 words of something. (And it wasn't my wedding day that I missed—I wrote before the ceremony. Planning!)

I think there's a need for a book that gives practical, real-world advice about the entire thesis/dissertation process. Moreover, I believe (based on both observations and data) that the way the thesis/dissertation process gets approached can be unhealthy. Grad school as a phase of life can be unhealthy, because of the message—implicit or explicit—that the only thing that matters is doing as much work as you can in a very compressed time period, to prepare yourself for a life of doing more work.

This ignores everything we've observed over the past few years (and the continually growing research literature!) about wellness and self-care. Taking care of yourself isn't something that only starts after grad school. It starts now. Or, better, yesterday! Approaching the process of writing your thesis or dissertation while remaining committed to taking care of yourself and your needs is vital.

Finally, I'm pretty confident that there's a need for affordable, accessible resources, that don't bury advice in mounds of BS or the mark-ups you have to pay for so many of the books you're required to purchase as part of your education. This is why this book in digital format should never cost any student more than $2.99 (print copies prices are a separate matter, and are harder for me to predict, so I will mainly encourage e-book purchases), and if you download it for free, I honestly don't care. I'd rather you have access to it than not. But hey, if you want to kick the $2.99 or whatever my way, cool. I'll buy myself some tea.

Like, not expensive tea. Just a few bags, maybe. But I'll be *damned happy* with that tea, if it reminds me that I may have helped somebody succeed on their educational journey.

Anyway, in this book I'll offer advice and observations, based on my years of offering other students advice and observations. I will try to keep any individual section brief, and do my best not to be boring. I want this to be something where you can open it, find a section that seems to fit your current struggle, and read a few paragraphs or pages to give you ideas or inspiration before getting back to work.

You can read it front-to-back, I guess (such as that's going to be meaningful, in an e-book format...). That's not how I'd use it, but one of the things I hope you take away from this book is that anybody who gives you advice about writing, and who tells you that, "This is how I do it, so this is how you have to do it," is deluded. They are (again) full of crap, they are trying to build their brand, and they really don't care whether or not you succeed.

I'm still not denying that I'm full of crap, but my "brand" is "A person who loves writing and who wants to help others love writing and become better writers." I'm a college professor who saw a need and decided to write a book, and the entire purpose of that book is to help you succeed. It is not a detailed description of "how to write a thesis." That field's been plowed plenty of times already, and I'm not interested in trying to shove some new crop-metaphor into it.

In terms of organization, the book has three main sections, each of which gets broken down into lots of more bite-sized (mainly a few paragraphs to a few pages) chunks.

In the first section, I'll talk about your preparation. A thesis or dissertation requires that you read, and organize, and oh yeah—figure out what the hell you're going to be writing about. I've got a lot to say about preparation, and thinking carefully about things like committee selection and staying organized is important throughout the thesis-writing process.

Then I'll talk about the actual writing. Here's the short form:

Sit down and freaking write.

Or stand, I guess. Hemingway wrote standing up, didn't he? You could be cool like Hemingway. I'm pretty sure Brandon Sanderson also writes standing up, but he's way too nice a guy to swear as much as I do when it comes to writing, whereas Hemingway was... Hemingway.

In the last section, I'll talk more generally about

managing the thesis process. At multiple points in this book, I emphasize that the thesis is an *exercise in project management*. The thing is, there are different types of "project management." There's the management of this "project" that is your thesis or dissertation, in terms of deadlines and meetings and administrivia. Then there's the management of the project that is you. As in, your life, your health, and your well-being. Both of those "projects" are important, but grad students tend to not treat them as even remotely equivalent. In fact, most grad students kind of get it backward.

Finally, a note about profanity.

If there is one thing that is almost universally agreed-upon, it's that the process of writing the thesis or dissertation will, from time to time, suck. The level of suckage will vary from a minor annoyance to an all-out assault on your self-esteem and identity. You will become frustrated. You will question your life choices. You will curse the teacher from third grade who praised you for being so smart, and told you that you were one of those "special students" who would go on to college and beyond and do great things, but who neglected to tell you that "great things" involved a kind of hard work that your third-grade brain had no means to comprehend. There will be days when you cannot stand the thought of opening the files that contain your thesis, when the idea of looking at another article fills you with the kind of dread that really ought to be reserved for a nightmarish high school reunion attended only by you, and people who dumped you to hook up with your best friend.

You have to let that frustration out. One of my favored mechanisms has always been swearing. Out of respect to the many folks who prefer their pedagogy to be profanity-free, though, I've stripped most of the sweariness out of the main text. It now lives in the final section of the book, tucked away in a dark little corner that allows me to pretend I'm being polite by hiding all the "bad words" in a place that doesn't gatekeep anything vital.

Anyway, let's get started. In a lot of ways, that's the hardest part.

PART THE FIRST: PREPARATION

No one sits down and cranks out a thesis or dissertation. (I'm going to stop saying both now, and simply write "thesis." It's easier.) You must plan. You must gather information. You must make decisions about how to proceed, what kinds of meetings need to occur, what resources you may have to obtain—lots of specific, nuanced things that I can't foresee, that you will have to deal with.

One thing that I can foresee is that the more work you do before you start writing, the easier the writing will be. You need to plan and organize, but don't over-plan and paralyze yourself into inactivity. You need to be able to recognize when you've got everything together and need to just start writing.

Here are a few things to consider, prior to starting the writing process.

You Are the Project Manager

It's possible you're in a field where a graduate degree gets you a job in which you never have to write anything like a thesis again. If so, the question of "Why?" may come to mind for you. As in, "Why am I writing a thesis?" The answer is that what you're about to do is more than just "write a thesis." You're going to develop life skills that will serve you throughout your career.

Whatever job(s) you end up with, you will have to manage projects. Success in life involves project management, because being able to figure out how to approach a project and execute a plan are central to just about everything. And you may have had a few projects in the past, maybe group projects or semester-long papers or whatnot, that tested you.

I would bet good money that none of those gave you the project management experience your thesis will. Here, you figure out the plan of attack. You create the timeline. You decide who you want to work with (and to some extent, how). You do the writing. You figure out how to address criticisms. You schedule the meetings. You. You, you, you, you, YOU.

I don't say this to scare you. I totally didn't cackle like a madman as I finished that last paragraph.

Promise.

At each stage you're building competencies that translate to the world outside academia. There's more than just writing. There's also literature searching, organizing, coordinating schedules, communicating with supervisors, and if you're in a discipline where you're collecting data as part of your thesis, you may have undergraduate or graduate research assistants to supervise. You may have to navigate an institutional review board (IRB) process. You will end up with a final written product that reflects much more than the typing of words on your laptop. It will demonstrate that you can undertake a large-scale project and carry it through to completion.

And it will probably be the first of many large-scale projects you'll do. No two will be exactly alike, but all of them will build on the core skill set that helps you write and defend your thesis.

~

Topic Selection

When I taught in a Master's program, I started every fall asking first-year graduate students what they were interested in researching for their thesis. Every year, at least 50% had no idea. They got into the field because they found it interesting, but asking what little "slice" they wanted to spend a chunk of the next two years researching?

It wasn't even a fair question. I knew it wasn't a fair question. Didn't keep me from asking it, though.

I'm a jerk that way.

I say that it wasn't a fair question because when you start graduate school, you begin a journey. You have left the world of undergraduate education, which tends to be broad (even once you've selected your major), and moved into the niche that will define you as a professional. But that niche, it turns out, isn't very niche-like. It's also broad—and ambiguous, and filled with conflicting ideas and findings, and you will soon realize that you have no idea what you don't know. Moreover, you don't know what your *chosen field* doesn't know, that might be of value for you to research.

I asked the "jerk" question the first week because we had a two-year program. I asked the question, and made a point of noting ideas that could turn into thesis topics as we held class that first semester, to help students find the thing that made them go, "Yes, I want to learn more about that. I want to graduate knowing a lot about *that* thing *right there*."

I had a colleague who told students that one of the best predictors of students finishing their theses was finding a topic they're passionate about. This was based on anecdotal observations, but between his years of mentoring students and my own, I think he was right. The plural of "anecdote" is indeed not "data," but the combined forty-plus years of experience we had advising theses seems pretty data-like to me.

Find something that you love reading and talking about. When you're done with your degree, people who under-stand graduate training may ask you about your thesis. If you're passionate about it and chose something you can communicate, those conversations (or, you know, "inter-views") will tend to go well.

"But Morrie, that's not how things work in my program. I don't get to choose…"

If you're in a strict "mentorship" program, where you got admitted to work with a specific faculty member, you may not get/have to choose your topic. If that's the case, though, you can still find a way (in most cases) to tailor your thesis to the kind of work your mentor does.

That wasn't how it worked in our program. I mentored students because they decided that their style of working fit best with my style of mentoring, or because I happened to know something about the area they wanted to research, or because I like dogs and it was important that they not have to work with someone who did not like dogs. Whatever. The point is, students had the option of choosing who would chair their thesis, and what their topic would be.

There's nothing wrong with either model. Just know what you're getting into. Your first step, in any case, is to figure out what you're going to study. Find your topic. Nothing else can happen until that does.

~

Build Your Personal Brand

Who do you want to be? This question connects to the selection of your topic, but goes beyond it in a way that made me want to break it out for emphasis.

In your discipline, there are probably lots of ways to build a professional identity. There are specializations within specializations, and multiple options to define and describe yourself. At the moment, you're a graduate student, but that phase of your life only lasts two to five years.

That may seem like a long time. It isn't.

The thesis is the first opportunity you really have to think about what gets talked about as your "personal brand" (see Poeppelman & Blacksmith, 2014, for a somewhat early treatment of this idea, or just do some searching). You've probably heard about branding in other contexts, maybe even from advisors and career counselors interested in your future development. For organizations, branding has to do with becoming recognizable for a particular service or product. When you hear the word "Crest," for example, what do you think of?

Most likely, you thought about toothpaste. The Crest brand is associated with oral hygiene, and their most recognizable products get squeezed out of tubes.

The quicker the association between a company and what it makes or does, the stronger its brand recognition is, and the more successful its branding efforts have been.

You are your brand. You are developing the knowledge and skills that will let you bring something unique and valuable to your future employers. The thesis will probably be the first large-scale, tangible product related to your professional identity. What do you want people to find out about you, when they Google your name? (There's also the question of what they can already find out about you if they Google your name, but that's another conversation entirely.)

I mean, they will. Prospective employers check everything about you. But that's after they review your vita/résumé, which may have your thesis prominently displayed. This is more true for a vita, because academics care a whole lot about that type of thing, but still—employers hiring someone of your academic training may (should?) be interested in what interests you.

You are building your brand right now, so consider what your thesis topic tells people about you. Pay attention to how you might talk about it during interviews for your first job. At that point, much of what you've got to offer is your education, including both the content and the project management skills you got from your thesis. After the first job, your body of professional work should speak more loudly. But early on, the identity deriving from your thesis can be a powerful thing. Use it well.

∼

Read the F(riendly) Manual

The abbreviation "RTFM" is used in various fields, and the "F" often doesn't stand for "Friendly." Because I'm trying to use my "responsible adult" vocabulary, though, here we are: read the friendly manual.

That manual, of course, is whatever handbook/guide-book/web page/program requirements your program gives its students, which its students then proceed to pile other (physical or virtual) things atop for the next few years. I'll keep using the term "manual," because it fits with my juvenile allusion to profanity that comes from using "RTFM," but be aware that different programs call it different things.

I'm assuming your program has such a manual. If they don't, ask your advisor or the lead departmental administrative assistant (because they know everything!) what resources are available to help students plan for and conduct their thesis.

Whatever you find, read it. Now is the time. In that manual/handbook/whatever should the requirements for your thesis, an outline of the major sections, and a description of how the thesis process runs. There should be key deadlines as well. Flag them and put them in the calendar in your phone/on your computer. If you have to submit a prospectus (a brief summative document outlining the rationale for your thesis and how you intend to conduct it, required by some programs but not others), make note of the date it has to be submitted. If there is a deadline by which you have to defend in order to walk in graduation, flag the hell out of it.

The manual (or its equivalent) gives you a lot of information that you ought to know. Putting it off until later is a nice way to create extra work for yourself. And trust me—you don't need any more than you've got!

You can actually use a manual side-by-side with this book, if you like. I'll give a lot of advice, and as you read each section on mechanics in this book, find the comparable information in your program's materials. Decide for yourself how much of my advice applies and how much doesn't. The mechanics are often highly program-specific, so I offer general advice—but you need to be thinking about those specifics as you move through the process.

~

Find a Chair

Unless you plan on doing your thesis in Hemingway/Sanderson mode, you want a chair with good lumbar support. Everything else is secondary. Adjustable height, reclining, head-rest—none of it's as important as good lumbar support. The ones with the little pump that lets you inflate and deflate the lumbar are my favorite.

A section on office chairs would be kind of short, right? Goofy introductions aside, although finding a comfy chair in which to sit while you write is important (I negotiated for a good chair when I got my most recent job, and it was one of the smartest things I did during that negotiation process), I'm obviously talking about your thesis chair. That'd be your main advisor, also known as the person who will help shape you as a writer, also known as the person whose name you will curse on no fewer than thirty occasions but whom you may later consider naming a child after.

When I discussed selecting a topic, I talked about whether you were in a strict mentorship program; if you are, skip this section. You don't need to hear about how to choose your thesis chair, because your thesis chair has been chosen for you. Instead, take the opportunity to go to Ikea and test out their "Markus" chair. You're in grad school, so you can't afford a truly high-end office chair, but the Markus is a good chair. I've got one in my home office. Or skip Ikea and just do some searching and testing of your own. There are other well-reviewed options at around the same price point, and none of them are the over-priced, over-hyped mess that you get with Herman Miller chairs.

Anyway...

If you have the option of choosing your thesis chair/advisor, choose wisely. You need someone who can provide you with feedback, support you, and help you stay on-task.

The ideas of feedback, support, and keeping you on-task are not actually separable, as far as it goes, and all of them kind of converge on that word in the middle of the list: support.

That is one of the chair's primary roles. Now, chairs will think about what it means to "support" a grad student in different ways. To some, it's the financial support that comes from having the student working in their lab, doing research related to a grant they hold, and getting funding off that grant. That is "support," after a fashion. But for a lot of students, the support they need has less to do with their financial situation and more to do with the complexities of graduate school. Some students need a more empathic form of support, and some need less empathy and more oversight/management. Everyone who chairs any number of theses develops a mentorship style that reflects the type of support they tend to give. Not everyone who chairs theses can easily articulate what that looks like, though.

In what is almost a mantra for this book, and certainly

comes up a lot when I'm talking about preparation, you should ask other grad students what it's like to work with different faculty members. Ask how supported they felt working with their thesis chair, and how that support happened. This is a key relationship, so independent of working styles, knowing about your chair's general interaction style and how you are likely to be supported by them is something to consider.

That's the "squishy" side of things, to some extent. To move away from the squish, it's kind of important that your chair maybe knows a little bit about your topic, content-wise —but that's not always critical.

Your thesis chair is someone who can speak most directly to your work habits and quality, when the time comes to give out a list of references. That makes the choice of a chair functional both in the short term and the longer term. I would recommend that you talk with different faculty members to figure out who will be the best fit for you. Things to think about or ask:

To what extent does the person require regular meetings? Or allow for them?

How quickly do they process drafts, or expect you to process them?

How do they prefer to provide feedback?

How would they describe their style of/approach to working with students?

To unpack a few of these, a little bit, here are things to keep in mind.

Some chairs want a standing meeting with each advisee, to make sure everyone makes progress. They will happily set deadlines, which you'd better meet.

Others will tell you that this is your project, so you need to set the meeting schedule. They will meet as often as you want (within reason; you are probably not this person's only advisee, after all), or maybe they will be just as happy handling drafts via email. There's nothing I personally have found that made the feedback process any easier than turning on "Track Changes" and marking up a document.

Some chairs will utilize departmental policy to guide how long they take to review your drafts. (Our thesis manual said advisors had up to two weeks to review any draft submitted.) Others will review them as soon as they are able.

I don't recommend asking a prospective chair, "So, how long should I expect to wait for feedback from you?" That doesn't do much to build a good working relationship.

Again, ask other grad students instead.

You should decide if you want a chair (a) whose working style is close to yours, so that it's easier for you to make progress and communicate with them, (b) whose working style is almost opposite yours, so you get experience working with someone whose expectations for how to get work done differ dramatically from your own, or (c) whose working style you'd like to emulate. Your inclination may be to ignore option (b), since it sounds like kind of a masochistic way to go through graduate school. Remember, though—this relationship is not the totality of graduate school, and in life you'll end up working for supervisors who think that the way you do things is wrong, and that you need to adopt their way instead. Plus, as one of my colleagues pointed out, working with someone whose style is different from yours gives you the opportunity to improve in areas where you are less developed, less experienced, and potentially even a little fearful. So option (b) has some real benefits.

Figuring out meetings, electronic feedback, how fast

they expect you to turn things around, and whether this is someone you would be comfortable working with for the next year or more are important. You don't want to ignore their domain knowledge, so make sure you ask about whether this is a topic they'd be interested in chairing a thesis on. If the person who knows the most about your topic is someone who makes you viscerally uncomfortable, maybe you should talk to the person who knows the second-most about the topic. Expert number one could then become a member of your committee.

You want someone with whom you can work. Listen to the way prospective chairs talk in class, look at what kind of feedback they provide on assignments (you will get a LOT of feedback from your chair, so make sure the feedback they give is feedback you can cope with), and talk to other graduate students. As is true with so many things, if there are "land mines" that come with working with particular faculty, your fellow students will almost always tell you.

And perhaps most importantly...

You want someone who will hold you to a high standard. I once had a student tell me that after I gave them feedback on their first short paper, they cried. Not a happy kind of, "Oh, at last, someone who is willing to give me feedback!" I wasn't mean (I don't think...)—I just tell students what they need to work on and why the way they've presented information isn't necessarily the best way. The sheer volume of feedback can, I guess, be overwhelming.

The student said, "I read your feedback and I cried... and I knew then that I had to have you as my thesis chair."

This is NOT actually how I recommend choosing a chair. I worked with the student, and they did one of the most interesting theses I've chaired since I started teaching

—then went on to be very successful. I hope (but am not sure) that I didn't make them cry again.

Nobody wants to make students cry. Nobody worth working with, at least.

The basic idea that student had—to work with someone who would hold them to a high standard—is a good one. Most faculty members who are qualified to chair a thesis will hold you to a high standard, though, so expect to be pushed. Expect to be told you can do better. Expect, if you half-ass something, to get called on it. Up your game! That's why you came to graduate school—to get better at everything it takes to be a professional in your field. In almost every field that matters, being able to write well is part of being successful.

~

Choose Your Committee

Although you don't have to pick a thesis committee before you start writing, it's good to strategize early on. Knowing to whom you will be presenting your project may shape how you build the document. A few factors should play into your decisions about committee composition.

The first goes back to reading the (friendly) manual. Your department or university probably has requirements for who can be a committee member, and sometimes the composition of your committee. I don't recall any required aspects of my thesis committee; I just picked a few faculty members from my program and moved ahead. For my dissertation committee, though, I had to have someone from outside my program. And I've got a friend who didn't review the full committee requirements, and whose chair also didn't do so, and scheduled a proposal meeting short one committee member. This could have ended very badly (as in, not passing the proposal), but they managed to find a way to correct the error. It was close, though, and reading the manual would have kept it from ever happening.

Usually, the manual's requirements will be something like "faculty member, or individual with a relevant degree and sufficient expertise to make a substantive contribution, blah blah blah." In our program, faculty members (full-time and adjunct) were fine. Individuals from the community were fine, but had to have at least a Master's degree, and were required to submit a résumé to the Department Chair for approval. The thesis chair had to be a full-time faculty member from within the department, and the Department Chair was officially a member of every committee (but almost never attended any meeting for which they were not a formal member).

You want committee members who will help you make the document better. How do you find such people? You look for expertise. You should know a lot about your topic area by the time your thesis makes its way into the hands of your committee members. Your chair should either (a) already know a lot about your area or (b) know almost as much as you do, by virtue of having read and re-read your document. Are there areas of the document that you're not as confident about, things that might limit its potential contribution down the road? If so, seek out committees members to help fill those gaps. Maybe it's a substantive area (e.g., part of the research literature that's tangential to what you are doing, but that might raise questions about your conclusions if not addressed) and maybe it's a method-ological area (e.g., stats that aren't your thing or your chair's, that you want to make sure you're using correctly).

If other faculty members have read your writing and given you feedback that helped you improve, you should have them on your committee as well (if they aren't already chairing it, of course). What you specifically don't want, though, are faculty members who have read your work, slapped a grade on it for a class, and given it back to you without much in the way of commentary.

Does it sound nice, to think that you might have a committee member who won't ask you questions, or who may come up with a throw-away question and then spend the rest of your meeting checking their phone? Does the idea of a non-threatening, uninvolved committee member appeal?

IT SHOULDN'T.

You are doing something that matters to you, spending months of your life on this project. Do NOT stack your committee with poly-degreed lumps of flesh who sit there and nod and ask the occasional "Are you still awake?" question. The thesis is not about Easy Mode. Easy Mode is Doing. It. Wrong. You want committee members to challenge you (in a good way) and help you see the holes in your arguments, the flaws in your logic. If you don't find them at the committee stage, your entire thesis may be doomed.

And that's not hyperbole. There's nothing worse than sitting in a final meeting and hearing, "Boy, I wish we'd thought of that sooner. It would've changed everything!"

Well, I guess there's one thing that's worse: "Sorry. You did not pass your thesis defense."

Start by talking to your chair about who might be good to include. Then talk to potential committee members. It is really that simple. Go and talk to each of the committee members to find out whether they're interested. The workload for committee members isn't generally onerous. Everywhere I've been, they get a copy of the document about two weeks prior to the meeting, read it, come in and ask questions about it, and vote. The time commitment to be a thesis committee member is often measurable in hours on two hands, including the time spent in meetings. At least, that's how it is for me.

When there is a university norm that says committee members are supposed to read and provide feedback on drafts prior to the ones that get distributed, their workload goes up. But most faculty members, in my experience, are happy to sit on committees. It's a form of teaching, it's a form of service, it helps us read about new directions in scholarship, and it gives a break from our routine.

You should (again!) talk to other students. You are not the first person to choose a committee, after all. Students who have already proposed or defended their theses can tell you what it's like to have various folks on your committee. Is one of them the guy who sits back in his chair, leans against the wall, and plays with the cord from the wall-phone that nobody knows why it's still in this room when everybody has cell phones? Then he looks at you and asks some terrifyingly penetrating question that cuts through everything you're arguing like a hot knife through ice cream?

(You thought I was going to say "butter," didn't you? Hah! Consider this a lesson within a lesson. Avoid cliché phrases like "hot knife through butter." They're lazy. If you change them up, your writing becomes more interesting and memorable. Somebody stabbing ice cream is an image that lingers.)

Your peers will also be the first to tell you if there are faculty members who simply do not get along and should never be on the same committee. Some folks, if you put them on a committee (or in a room...) together, can get ugly.

In some programs—and I hope you're not in one of these—there's a lot of in-fighting amongst the faculty, a lot of competitiveness. Graduate students can get caught in the crossfire, and you do not want to be in the crossfire, especially if one of the people lobbing hate across the table is your chair. If you invite your chair's nemesis (what? You think only superheroes have those?) to be on your committee, you open yourself up to all kinds of avoidable pain.

Your chair may be used to these kinds of interactions, and most faculty don't like speaking ill of other faculty, so may or may not warn you off those kinds of potential conflicts. Students can and will tell you about weird or unpleasant dynamics to avoid.

Now, there's another way that disagreement among committee members can manifest, and it's not nearly as painful. I don't recommend trying this without verifying with multiple students that it works, but when it works it can be really entertaining.

If you have two committee members who are friends, but come at your discipline from different perspectives, having them on your committee can end up with protracted stretches of the meeting in which you are not being forced to answer questions or defend your work. Instead, you may find yourself watching them argue back and forth, using your thesis as a springboard to continue discussing something that they've probably discussed in various contexts several times in the past.

Any time your committee is talking to each other, the pressure feels like it's off you. Keep paying attention, though, because if you just sit back and let them talk, they may find a common ground and come back at you with a question fueled by both of them at once!

You want to retain control of the meeting, so you

shouldn't let discussions among members go too long. If it does happen, and it's a genial kind of discussion, let them go for a couple of minutes and then, when they pause, try something like this:

"I think those are both really interesting ways to look at what I'm describing. Dr. A, I think your perspective fits really well with [this here thing that you wrote about on page whatever], where Dr. B, I think that [some other stuff that you reviewed because you knew it was going to come up and besides, it's important] ties things together really nicely. I'm not sure that my thesis can fully disentangle those perspectives, but hopefully it provides new ways to move the conversation forward."

Note that this doesn't get you off the hook, and may lead to other questions, but one of the things that you ought to be doing in preparation for these meetings is figuring out what kinds of questions are likely to arise.

There are more benign things that it's helpful to know about potential committee members. For example, do any of your committee members have particular pet peeves? Is one professor such an adherent to the use of multiple regression that they bristle whenever a student wants to run an ANOVA? Is another professor notorious for finding every possible format and style issue, no matter how minor (and lingering on them)? If you put Dr. H on your committee, are you basically guaranteeing that at some point you'll have to deal with the question, "This is conceptually interesting, but what does it actually mean in the real world?" Every potential committee member has foibles and habits. Knowing about those allows you to prepare for how to respond to them, and will help your proposal/defense meetings run more smoothly.

~

Find Sources

At some point, after you've figured out your chair and all the other preliminary "stuff," you need to dig in and start doing research. Step one is finding sources. This ought to be easy. Right? And maybe for you it is. Maybe you know everything you need to know about locating articles and books and chapters. If so, you don't need this section. Go elsewhere.

Surprisingly (to me), a lot of students never get much instruction on how to find sources. So I'll give you a few basics, then leave you to your own devices.

If you're in graduate school, you're probably at a university (and if you're not physically at one, you're at least enrolled). If you're at a university, it probably has a library. You remember libraries? They're buildings with books and journals and magazines and newspapers inside. You sometimes see them in old movies.

The physical library is less important for what's in it than it is for who's in it. Any more, a lot of what you want can be obtained digitally, books included, through your library's website. You may be in an online program that makes a brick-and-mortar library completely impractical (though I would point out that if you're near a city of any size, that city probably has several libraries which may have access to academic journals). It's the people in the library who matter, particularly your reference librarians.

Reference librarians are wonderful human beings who love to help people find things. Find out who your reference librarian is (your university may have several; if so, find out which one works most closely with your department) and schedule a meeting. In person, if possible; because libraries mainly get used by people who want a quiet place to study, librarians don't get asked as many questions as they used to. If you become not just an email correspondent, but an actual face and voice, you will stand out and be more likely to get help quickly. You have a lot to do, to finish your thesis; identifying people who can help you get it done is important.

For the rest of it, there's the internet. I won't tell you how to use your local library's system. You'll find that most of it is based on the kinds of search engines you've been using for years, but with weird clunks and bumps and rules that most commercial search engines have long since abandoned. Still, it's a set of search engines, and you can't break it, so play around. Find what you can. Then, when you hit articles that your library doesn't have access to, figure out what to do next.

One option is requesting articles via interlibrary loan. If you search your university's website, you'll find a means of requesting items that are not in your school's holdings. Generally, you'll fill out a form, it goes to your friendly reference librarian, and they find a school or public library that has what you want. If it's an article, the other school can often get it scanned and emailed to you in a couple of days. If it's a book, you may have to wait for it to be scanned, or for real "vintage" sources, mailed.

Get to know your reference librarian, and get to know your library's databases, and when there are items that are outside your library's ability to obtain, remember that there are other options.

If you're not patient, though, head back to the internet. Register on ResearchGate.net. It's social networking for researchers, and you'll sometimes find articles there that your library doesn't have. If you can find the authors on

ResearchGate, you can also request a full-text copy from them, even if it's not posted for download.

Google scholar (scholar.google.com) is another great resource that you probably know. Through it, you can sometimes find copies of papers your library may not have access to, which have been posted to some website or other. These are often university websites where a professor has posted the article for a class, sometimes in violation of copyright laws. I won't endorse violating copyright laws or taking advantage of the hard work of researchers, but I will say that there is very little that a determined user can't eventually turn up. And that's before we talk about sci-hub. Which we won't talk about. Because I think one of the rules of sci-hub is that you don't talk about sci-hub. So I'm not.

When searching for sources, a common question is, "How many?" As in, "How many sources do I really need, for my thesis?" The short answer is that there is no "right" number of articles/sources. Gather information until you feel like you can write about the topic (sleepy terriers). Then read some more. If you have been told, by another student or some other book about writing theses or even by your chair, that you need some minimum number of articles before you start writing, ignore that number. Or if you're not going to ignore it, double it. If you stop reading when you get to the minimum number of articles you have to include, you will almost always leave out something important that you would have found if you'd read just one more article. And if you're wondering whether you have enough articles yet? Just asking the question means that you don't.

You should gather piles and piles (these can be virtual piles; I don't discriminate) of information. If you're gathering hard copies, keep them organized. Invest in file folders and paperclips and whatever else you need to make sure you know where to find what you need. If you're gathering everything digitally, for the love of all that is holy, BACK IT ALL UP.

Cloud-based storage systems like Google Drive, Dropbox, and OneDrive are vital, any more. Backing up anything important to a cloud drive, and your hard drive at home, and an external SSD, and probably somewhere else, is important.

One other thing—and I'll come back to this later on. I'm not sure where generative AI will be in its lifespan when you read this, but right now, it is TERRIBLE for finding sources. I have seen it literally make up citations. So don't ask ChatGPT or whatever the AI flavor-of-the-week is to find you sources. Use a regular search engine, skip the AI summary at the start, and look for original sources. That's what you need. And if you do get an AI's help to find sources, do yourself a favor and make sure that they exist.

Finally, always download/procure the original source if you can. Don't trust anyone else's summary of it—human or AI. Reading the original source allows you to make connections that reviewing someone else's summary just won't give you.

∾

And Now, READ

No matter your discipline, you must read. Read anything you can get your hands on related to your topic. Read recent articles. Read books. If you're in a field where meta-analyses get done, read meta-analyses. If step one is "Find lots and lots of things to read," step two would be, "Read them."

While reading, pay attention to things in parentheses

(like this!). It's easy to train your brain to overlook or ignore things that happen inside parentheses. You probably already did; in the last chapter, when I was talking about how many sources to find, I tacked on a parenthetical to one of the sentences that mentioned a kind of dog. If you didn't linger on the parenthetical because it felt like some irrelevant aside or random example, you may not remember it being there at all. But it's there. Feel free to go check.

The thing with information in parentheses is that the sentence ought to read just fine without the parenthetical information. This is true for both substantive information and in-text citations, which some style guides (e.g., APA style) encourage/allow to be presented in parentheses. You tuck information about the author(s) and the year in parentheses so that it's there, if anybody cares about it, but doesn't disrupt the flow of the sentence. That makes it easy to ignore things in parentheses. In other styles, you end up with the citations removed from the text entirely, and just flagged with an endnote or footnote, which is even easier to ignore!

You need to read parentheticals, or at least notice them, because they help you expand your literature review and better understand the author's thought processes. Who gets cited in this area? Are you reading their work? If not, that's a problem. Find out who the big names are, then read them. Then read the people they cite. Then read the people who cite them.

Don't just read, either. Read and take notes. Highlight, insert comments, do whatever it takes. This is not passive reading; you are actively seeking information to help you build the case for your thesis. You will (and we'll get to this) have some number of arguments that are central to what you want the reader to take away from reading your thesis.

As you read through the various articles and chapters and reports and so forth, you're looking for the pieces that will form your arguments. Because those pieces can be found anywhere in the article, this also means you need to avoid the temptation to just read the abstract or the summary.

Keep good track of what you read and your main take-aways from each source. Again, this is active reading.

One aspect of active reading is figuring out what the mechanism is that you're going to use, to track what you're learning. Are you going to start a spreadsheet? A fresh Word document for your notes? An actual physical notebook (SO RETRO) where you write things down? Do something to keep the reading active. It's important.

Having said all that?

Pace yourself. Reading—especially if it's active reading —is a "high cognitive load" kind of activity. You can and will get fatigued. Read an article or chapter, then take a break. Pet some puppies. Feed your fish. Hug your significant other. Do some squats. Then come back and read something else. Sitting and reading five or ten articles at a stretch is not a sign of virtue or dedication. It's a sign that you are pushing yourself too hard and not taking breaks that your brain and body both need.

~

Keep YOU in the Work

I mentioned the "personal brand" earlier, but after you spend a ton of time reading other people's writing, it's kind of easy to lose your unique perspective. After you read, and read, and read, you need to step back and remind yourself why you're doing this thesis. Remind yourself of your perspective and what's important to you. What's your story? It won't just be about summarizing and quoting everybody else; it will be about what you have to offer that's new and exciting. *Your* story. *Your* brand. Which you will lose sight of if you endlessly quote what everyone else says.

The more you quote, the less the thesis is about what you have to say, and the more the thesis is about what fifty or eighty or however many other authors have already said. And anybody who wants to know what all those other authors said? They can go read those other authors. A reader who has chosen to sit down and open your thesis wants to know what you have to say.

So... don't make your thesis about what everybody else has said. Make it about how you interpret and build upon what they've said.

Over-quoting isn't the only place you can lose your perspective. Remember that you are not obligated to use everything that you read. As with any domain in the universe, some of what you read on your topic will be excellent, some of it will be fine, and some of it will be steaming piles of Irish wolfhound excrement. So be critical; ask yourself how what you're reading is relevant to your thesis. If you can't answer that question in two minutes or less, set that source aside.

Don't throw it away, though. Just don't feel like you have to use it RIGHT NOW.

Make brief notes while reading about what you find useful—either on the article or in a separate spreadsheet/document. Saying, "I know I read something about [whatever], but I can't remember which source it was in," and then staring at the pile of physical articles or the directory full of pdf files, will create unpleasant queasiness in your gut.

It's pretty much guaranteed to happen. But the more attention you pay to how each source contributes to the story you plan on telling, the less going back and searching you'll have to do. Which leads, quite naturally, to more consideration of organization.

~

Organize Your Material as You Read

There's a special kind of queasiness that comes from, "Where the hell did I read that one important fact that makes this whole section make sense?" To avoid it, you need to find an organizational system that makes sense for you. For example, index cards (or an app that simulates their important characteristics) can be an invaluable organizational tool, as can the spreadsheet or Word document I mentioned earlier. You're about to put together a document with a lot of moving parts. You will build an argument that forms the centerpiece of your thesis, supporting that argument with what you've read.

Each article (or chapter, or book) that you read contains elements that may be relevant to different pieces of your argument. Early on, you have a singular purpose: learn as much as you can before you start writing. As you move forward, though, you'll go back to your sources with specific goals. Whether it's building your core argument or finding a measure or whatever, you end up needing different sources for different reasons.

Say a source gives you good information about how to define a concept and what kinds of factors might affect that concept. (Writing in language broad enough to apply to multiple disciplines is harder than I thought...) When writing about that concept, you may have a section on Definitions, one on Precursors, another on Outcomes, and so forth. You can use index cards as one way of keeping everything organized; you can do each point on its own index card, or you could do a card that contains source information for everything about "Definitions," or whatever works for you. The same can be done with tabs in a spreadsheet. I know plenty of writers who use colored sticky notes on a wall or white-board in their office.

The reason I personally like index cards is that they can be organized and re-organized. Yes, you can cut-paste within a document. Control-X and Control-V (yes, I'm a Windows person...) are wonderful. But sometimes, you need to take a step back and look at the overall layout of your argument. What comes first? What next? Is there any reason to try a different order? What if I moved this idea ahead of that one? Do these concepts need to stay separate, or would it make more sense to combine them? Add in that the act of physically moving something activates different parts of your brain than shuffling things around on your screen, and the cards offer yet another bonus.

Index cards can be useful at multiple stages. For example, with this book I started by making a list of the topic areas I wanted to write about. Then I wrote about them. Then I took the index cards with the topic areas on them and figured out what the best way to organize everything would be. Then I shared the book with an alpha reader (someone who reviews a VERY early draft) and, after she and I finished going through her edits, we sat down on the floor, spread out the cards, and re-organized everything again.

The more interconnected concepts and ideas you're dealing with, the more helpful index cards can be. They give you the freedom to move things without the self-loathing that often accompanies changing material you've worked really, really hard just to get on the page in the first place.

You don't have to use index cards. Everything I just described could be done with sticky notes. In addition, when I was working on the final drafts of this book, I shifted to Scrivener writing software. Scrivener gives you an "index card" view of your document, based on sub-sections, and you can just move the virtual index cards the way my alpha reader and I did on my office floor. So you've got options. I would strongly, *strongly*, encourage you to pick one, and use it!

~

To Outline?

I'm not going to tell you that you have to outline your thesis. I will, however, tell you that not-outlining your thesis can make it way more difficult to write.

I hated outlines when I first learned them, way back in fifth grade. I never saw the point. Why make an outline when you could just WRITE? It didn't make sense to me.

Then I got to sixth grade, was assigned my first five-page paper, and learned to my ever-lasting horror what it felt like to sit down with a bunch of sources and no plan the afternoon before a paper was due.

Man. Did I wish I had an outline for that paper about Romania. Would've made things so much easier.

These days, my outlining is not as rigorous as what I first learned with, with major headings and sub-headings and all those little rules. I do bullets. With this book, obviously, there are three major headings: preparation, writing, and project management. So I wrote those down, bulleted out the major points in each section, and started writing.

Again, it doesn't matter HOW you organize your material before you start writing. But you need to have some kind of organization. An outline is one non-terrible option.

~

Know Where You're Starting (and Where You're Going!)

Sometimes, the correct place to start writing is with the introduction to your lit review. Not always, though. Where you start depends on your writing style and the argument/hypotheses you are trying to build.

In my "perfect world," everybody would start by writing their introduction, because a well-crafted introduction serves as an executive summary of the logic and layout of the entire document. It hooks the reader and sets up everything that comes after. However, some folks hate the introduction, and feel like they need to be able to "see" the entire document before they can write the three to five paragraphs that set up the thesis. Either method works. To me, though, if you don't know where you're going well enough to write a coherent introduction, you may not be ready to start writing.

Of course, even if you write the introduction first, you will probably still go back and edit the hell out of it later.

What does a good introduction do, then? Well, consider the following:

It has long been understood that...

You start with a statement of a core problem.

In recent years, however...

Things change.

The present thesis will argue...

Hey, look—it's about you! (Note that in some disciplines use of first-person language is fine, whereas in others, if you write in first-person you are a heathen and a cretin and clearly must have gone to some school whose mascot was Garth, the Talking Grit.)

First, the literature on [iggly boo] will be considered, followed by our current understanding of [farfel].

You then proceed to lay out, for the reader, the structure of your literature review. This is what's sometimes called an "advance organizer," or more colloquially, "Just a freakin' good idea, so do it." The former term, as you might guess, is more academically acceptable.

The latter's not wrong, though.

Remember that no matter your field/discipline, if you're writing a thesis, you are arguing for something. If you're in the sciences, you've probably got some number of hypotheses that you'll be testing. In that case, your review of the literature should focus on building the case for those hypotheses. Whatever your discipline, though, your thesis should intend to make some kind of contribution to the broader literature in your field.

You should be able to sum up the core of your thesis in one or two sentences. If you can't do that, you're definitely not ready to start writing, and you're probably going to have trouble focusing your review of the literature in a way that lets you make progress.

I've heard students say, "I'm really interested in job satisfaction." To which my response is often something like, "In what way?"

That's the nice form. In my head it may be a little more like, "Right, you and every manager worth a damn in the country, a reasonable number of organizational consultants, and researchers who have published over 35,000 papers on the topic." Studying job satisfaction is fine, but you need to have something to say about it that hasn't already been said 35,000 times.

Find what you have to say. You WILL NOT KNOW this to start with, and that's okay. Read broadly, take notes, write questions in the margins of papers, ask professors about your ideas. You will, through this initial process, triangulate on the issue or issues that you're most interested in, and be able to describe the purpose of your thesis in one or two sentences.

Those one or two sentences may take some work, but until you can get it to that stage, you don't have a strong enough focus to write a thesis.

When you do, though, the lit review really starts to take shape. Once you know what you want the main take-away from your thesis to be, you can figure out how to get there. If you don't know where you're going, though, it really doesn't make sense to take the car out of "Park".

If you know what you're ultimately arguing, you can figure out the pieces (whether they are variables, critiques, classic authors, or whatever) that you have to review in order to get to your target. You know what you have to read, and your reading can become more focused.

Without knowing what you're arguing—where your thesis is actually going—you will find yourself frustrated over and over again.

〜

Find Your Process

When I started drafting this book, I found myself typing variations on, "You could do this, or you could do that, or you could do something else entirely." That plays into my desire to be as minimally full of crap as possible. In that vein, one of the things I've learned by virtue of writing some ridiculous number of words (1,000/day for over 25 years—you do the math...) is that I cannot possibly guess what your writing process ought to be. I can give you examples of things that have worked for me, or for my students, but I cannot tell you what your process is. Only you can discover that.

You've written papers before.

God, I hope that's true. It's an assumption I'm working from in creating this book—that you have written at least brief papers in the past, and that the thesis is just a step (or leap) up the complexity ladder. It may not be true, though, and if you somehow made it through your undergraduate education without ever writing something more than 1-2 pages in length, I'm truly sorry. I know this can happen for some majors at some really big universities, where the classes are over-full and the professor doesn't have the time or TA support to read and grade 200 or 300 5-pages essays. If so, you may not have any idea what your writing process is, and you may be starting from scratch.

No matter how many papers you've written, reflecting on the best way to approach writing can be useful. With that in mind, I will describe what I mean by "writing process," and you can figure out for yourself what is likely to work for you. Everyone has a way in which they work best. Once you find that way, you can then use it to produce your highest-quality work. Here are a few things to think about in finding your way—your process.

When do you have the most energy? Are you a morning person? Or do you need a few hours to get up and get your head straight, then you do your best work in the afternoon? Or are you a night owl, and work best after everybody else has gone to bed, when distractions are fewest?

You want to identify the time of day when it's easiest for you to get work done. Then you need to set aside time during that window in which you are going to work on your thesis.

For me, I'm at my most productive in the afternoon and early evening. That's when writing comes easiest for me; I've gone to work, dealt with the emails and classes and meetings, and wrapped up. Then I get to write. It's easier for me because all the "normal" stuff has been taken care of. If there were fires to put out, they're out and I can write with minimal interruption. Sometimes I'll write earlier, if there's nothing on my schedule, and sometimes I'll come back to what I've been working on after 10 at night, to get a few more paragraphs or pages written.

Find a time when you know you can be productive and protect it. Do not schedule other things during the time you've set aside for your thesis. Do not let other students in your project group convince you that you need to meet during your thesis time; you will respect their thesis time, and they need to respect yours. The thesis needs to be a priority, and finding a time that is "thesis time" allows you to treat it as such. I can't tell you when that time needs to be— but I can tell you that you need. That. Time.

What's the right environment? Some people love having background music while they read or write, and others can't function with distractions. Stephen King has written about how he uses music while he writes. I just can't. If the TV is on, or there's music, or if I let myself open a browser, I'm pretty much screwed. For other people, if there isn't activity around them, they can't focus.

Do you need to be at home, by yourself? Or do you need to be somewhere like a coffee shop, away from the distractions of your house/apartment? There is, for each of us, an environment in which we're going to be most productive. Finding yours is part of your process.

What kind of goals should you set? Some people set a target word count, like my "1,000 per day" rule. I don't recommend that for a thesis. You need to look at what kinds of goals are realistic. These are both micro-level goals ("I need to find at least three articles to flesh out this section") and macro-level goals ("I want to propose by September 30"). And, as a friend pointed out to me, micro-level goals often exist *within* the macro-level goals!

If you're going to set timeline goals, make sure you set multiple. Just having a goal for when you want to propose or defend by won't do you any good if you don't have sub-goals for milestones within your writing process. What it will do—and I've seen this more times than I like—is have you panicking as that one uber-deadline draws near. You want to propose by September 30, but it's August 1 and you haven't finished your lit review! Your committee has to have the document two weeks ahead of time, which means that you have to have it in their hands by September 16, which is only a month and a half away! Where did the time go?!?

The time went where time always goes—to other things that had more immediate deadlines (or were more entertaining). If you don't create sub-deadlines for yourself, and hold yourself accountable, you will find yourself in panic mode.

Also, do not try to push the setting of deadlines off on your chair. That's not their job. This is your thesis. You are managing the project. You set the deadlines and you meet them.

If your chair likes setting deadlines, fine. But that's something you should figure out ahead of time.

Research is not necessarily linear, so writing may not be linear. If you figure out your methodology early on, write it up! Or write your hypotheses first. Or whatever. Your document will start with your lit review and proceed in what looks like a linear fashion to the reader, but almost no one writes every section in the order they appear in the final draft. If your process demands that you tackle a "later" section before an "earlier" one, do that. It's better to get that later section drafted while your brain is telling you to work on it than to sit and stare at the earlier one and make no progress on anything.

The harder the task, the easier the distraction. You need a process that helps you focus, because as a rule, difficult tasks intimidate us. If you can't figure out why your argument isn't working, it's hard to sit down, pick it apart, look at the order of your paragraphs and the points you're making, look at each paragraph and whether it makes its point well, look at each sentence and make sure that it's clear and doesn't obviously conflict with anything else you're arguing, and re-read key articles to make sure there's nothing you missed.

The easy thing to do is open a browser window and Google, "How to build an argument." Then get distracted reading about how, "This couple just had a screaming argument—and you WON'T BELIEVE what happens next!"

Then go check your email. Remember that it's your sister's birthday. Try to call, don't get her. Send a text, then go dig out a link to something you'd meant to tell her about. Go get another snack.

The more challenging something is, the more your instinct will be to put it off. Because right now, maybe you just don't have the energy. If you've developed a writing process that has you working in your best environment, at your best time of day, with everything weighted in your favor, you will have your best shot at avoiding (or overcoming) distractions.

That all being said...

You're (probably) not living in a monastery, having taken a vow to avoid worldly temptations. Finding a process that allows you to get work done does not require you to give up things you enjoy, or never waste time. It simply requires you to develop the discipline to make time and space to get work done, so that you can reward yourself later with the things you enjoy.

Not "later in life." Later today. Worst case, later this week. It's grad school, not solitary confinement.

∾

Make Consistent Progress

I could have put this topic in any section of the book, and it would have worked equally well. You see, the thesis is a pretty big undertaking. Getting it going is like push-starting a battleship, so once you get moving, you need to keep moving. Momentum is everything.

You may think I'm going to tell you to write every day, because I talk so much about my own habits. But remember, those are Morrie's writing habits. They are not your writing habits. If you can find time to actually write every day, and can write something useful every day, that's great. I've never been able to do "every day" on any given academic document. There's too much thinking involved, too much planning, too much organizing. I have to take days off from writing academic papers. Even when I was writing my dissertation, I didn't WRITE my dissertation every day.

And early on, you won't be doing much writing at all. But once you start making forward progress, the worst thing you can do is stop.

Even when you can't write, find something you can accomplish.

Maybe it's a day when you read and highlight an article. Or enter some articles in the document or spreadsheet you're keeping with your running reference list, so that you don't have to do all that crap at the end. Or let yourself freewrite for a little while about your thesis, to work through some of the problems you might be having. Maybe you do some of the pain-in-the-ass formatting that has to get done before you go to committee.

There's a lot you could be doing, to make progress. Especially early on, the act of writing is among your least important tasks. What matters is that you find the time to do something related to your thesis. Maybe you do it when you first wake up in the morning, so you know you've accomplished something meaningful. Anything you get done later suddenly becomes a bonus that gets you that much closer to being done! Or do it before you let yourself go to bed, and if there are nights when you sit bleary-eyed, staring at an article and re-reading the same paragraph for the third time, you may start finding times a little earlier in the day to make your progress.

It doesn't matter when you do it. It just matters that you do it.

Be consistent, but if you miss a day, don't beat yourself up. As you'll see later on, I definitely recommend taking days off!

～

All About the Argument

I've talked about "argument" a few times, but I want to wrap up this section by really drilling down into the idea.

All good academic writing, and much good business writing, is about argument construction. In your thesis, you build an argument for some theory or set of hypotheses or interpretation or whatever. In professional correspondence, you may build the argument for why a task should be done a particular way. You should always, when you sit down to write a document, have an idea of what you're going to argue.

Then, as you write, every section ought to contribute to the development of that argument.

This is why the planning stage is so vital, and it's why I use the word "argument" while writing about things like outlining and index cards. If you know the argument you're making you can work backward. You can figure out what literature you need to cite and what evidence you need to present, in what order, to make your argument make sense to the reader.

The argument is what allows you to build the one to two sentence summary I talked about earlier. If you can't articulate your core argument, you will have no idea where you're going, and therefore no idea where to start. You will write like a person drowning in the middle of the ocean, flailing one way and then the next, searching for a sign that you might have come in sight of land, or found something that floats—but you will eventually wear yourself out...

...at which point the metaphor gets really dark, so we'll just drop it.

Right now, what I'm doing is building the argument for building an argument. (So meta!) There are different ways to structure an argument and appeal to your reader. Most of what you'll be encouraged to use, depending on your discipline, are intellectual elements of argument. Present facts and figures, then extrapolate from those to what you want the reader to conclude.

There are also emotional elements of argument. Folks in the sciences (social and natural) don't use these quite so much, because they sometimes take the form of things like drowning as a metaphor for writing without self-direction. If you're only presenting intellectual arguments, you ought to recognize that you're failing to tap one of the tools that could make your argument more powerful by ignoring emotions.

The worst thing that happens, if you include an emotional element in your argumentation, is it gets cut later on. That's not a big deal. A lot of stuff will get cut later on.

Here's the really important thing with arguments, though: You ought to think about how to structure your entire paper so that the argument you want is the argument readers naturally find themselves reflecting on. This means paying close attention to how you set things up, then how you follow through. It means watching your transitions and doing all kinds of things that hand-hold your reader in the direction of your core argument. The better your initial structure, and the stronger you make the elements of your argument, the less likely the reader will pause and start asking those, "Why didn't you do…?" kinds of questions.

More on that, though, in Part Two.

Summary: Key Points on Preparation

Writing the thesis isn't just about producing an academic document. Think about what you want to learn from the *process* of writing your thesis, and appreciate that learning as well.

Find a topic that you care about, and that you want to associate yourself with. This is your chance to say something important, so say it!

You want a thesis chair who is knowledgeable and whose work style fits your needs. Most important, though, you want your chair to push you, and to care about the quality of the work you produce. Then you want a committee who can help you and your chair make the thesis even better.

Pay attention to little details now. At the beginning, they're just "little details." If you ignore them until closer to the end of your process, they will morph into "Gigantic freaking problems that I wish I'd paid attention to but who reads that crud anyway?" So, you know: read the manual.

Find sources. Find lots and lots of sources. Exploit the resources available to you through your university, like research librarians and databases.

Read, and read actively. Find ways to track and organize what you're reading about. Keep some number of documents or spreadsheets to help you track what you've read and why it's important. Organize your materials, and organize yourself. Find a writing process that helps you maximize productivity, and stick to it.

Remember that it's all about the argument. If you know what you want to argue, start from that point and work backward to figure out what literatures you'll need to review and how to set up the paper to really capture your reader's attention.

And all that being said?

You are preparing to write a thesis. It will be a meaningful part of your life for a while. It will not, and should not, **be your life**. Things will have to shift, you may have to change a few behaviors, but what you should not take away from my words is any admonition toward asceticism or intellectual self-flagellation. You are growing as you write your thesis, but you're not growing into someone different — just a slightly different you.

Hold onto what matters.

PART THE SECOND: WRITING

Let's get the biased part out of the way: I love writing. When I talk or write about writing, it's with a fondness that not everybody shares. I'm not going to apologize for loving the act of writing, but I'm also not going to rub it in your face, if you're frustrated or stymied or just a little bitter that you have to write a damned thesis.

There were plenty of times I didn't love my thesis, and even more when I didn't love my dissertation. When the writing wasn't as much fun as I knew writing could be, I did what you'll have to do: Keep writing anyway. Because you want to finish, and because you *will* finish.

In the introduction, I already gave you the only piece of writing advice that I think really matters:

Sit down and freaking write.

It's really that simple. That simple, and that complex, because when you write something you care about, you aren't just putting words on the page/screen. You're putting part of yourself there. You are creating something that will, eventually, get judged and graded. People who have taught you important things about life and your chosen profession will look at you, and look at your document, and furrow their brows, and ask you difficult questions.

That's later, but the possibility can distract or upset or befuddle you at any stage in the process.

Try not to let the "worst case scenario" occupy too much of your brain. Just recognize when you're getting stressed out and do something to relax. If possible, go somewhere that has puppies or kittens, and play with a small friendly animal for a little while. Having something cute and furry lick your face and nibble your fingers is a great way to let go of stress and get back in the right head-space for writing. Then bandage your fingers, return to your materials, and accomplish something.

You've got a thesis to write. Sit down and do something. Write a sentence. Write a paragraph. Write five pages. Do some formatting. Organize your references. And at the end of the day, be able to tell anybody who asks that yes, you made progress on your thesis, and yes, you feel good about it.

Because you should. Progress happens incrementally.

Here, then, are a few things I'd like you to think about and be aware of, as you start writing.

Telling a Story

A common metaphor for writing a thesis (or really, any research report) is that you're telling a story. The story metaphor is good in some ways, bad in others. Because it can break down a little when you start to pick at it, we'll look at it from a broad level.

What makes a story work? Think about books, movies,

or TV shows that you've appreciated. Or good research articles. You've probably read some of those.

Good stories generally do at least a couple of things well. The first is that they grab your attention. The second is that they change how we think about someone or something.

Hook the reader! When it comes to grabbing the reader's attention, good academic writing is no different than good fiction writing. Something has to happen. Something has to make the reader sit up and take notice. We call this "the hook." The hook captures the reader and drags them into your narrative.

For example...

It has long been suggested that lowland gorillas are peaceful creatures. Recent observational studies with lowland gorilla family units, however, have shown that not only are the animals not "peaceful," they can be highly organized in the pursuit of violence against other groups of gorillas.

That second sentence is totally made up, by the way. But if you were someone with an interest in lowland gorillas, wouldn't it make you want to keep reading?

You have, at most, a paragraph to convince readers that what you've written is worth their time. If you don't have the reader's attention within that first paragraph, you'll probably lose them. There is too much competition for attention, too much that we can read, watch, and do, for us to bother spending time on things that don't grab us.

Think back to any book, story, or TV show that you cared about. Pick up a research article that you found compelling. Read the first paragraph and identify the hook.

Go ahead. I'm not going anywhere.

Back? Okay, good. Now take something you've written and look at your first paragraph. Find the one or two sentences that justify the work you're doing, and justify anybody else caring about it. That is your hook.

Not all hooks are created equal. Your first attempt at a hook will probably be some ham-handed froofery that doesn't work at all. That's fine. The first paragraph is the hardest to write. I generally delete the first paragraph of anything I write, because it doesn't contain a good enough hook. Sometimes I delete the whole first page. Sometimes, it takes three or four or ten tries to get the first paragraph right.

Which is fine. That first paragraph is arguably the most important one in your paper. You know why you care about this topic; now you have to convince other people to care.

Try to be as objective as you can in answering this question: Why would anybody give a damn? If you can't answer that question, you've failed to set your hook.

And then, something changed! In fiction, we see changes in characters or changes in the world where they live. In your thesis, you have to challenge the reader's perception of some aspect of the world. It can be narrow or broad, but you need to build an argument that, at least potentially, changes the world around the reader.

If you're not challenging anything, what the hell is the point? If your thesis changes nothing, where is your contribution? Where are you, in the project? You're not just some scribe, writing down Thoughts about Stuff. You're a scholar working on a graduate degree, trying to make an impact on a field you're passionate about.

One of my personal writing heroes, John Bloom, once opined that no great writer has ever been a wimp (Briggs, 1991). That goes for fiction writers and non-fiction writers. You need to have something to say. You need to convince the reader that if you are right, they need to re-think some aspect of their world view. Something has to change.

When I tell students that they're telling a story, that's what I'm looking for. A hook, and the possibility of change.

All About the "Chunks"

You need to break your thesis into chunks—smaller, more achievable elements—to see regular progress. The literature in psychology makes it clear that the most motivating goals are difficult and specific. You can throw a citation to Locke and Latham in here—they're the ones who really made "difficult, specific goals" into buzzwords.

"Write a thesis" is certainly a difficult goal, but it's not very specific. A specific goal is, "Write a paragraph about this paper and how it relates to my argument" or "Do an outline for this section where I lay out the order of the sources I want to include."

Once you have a difficult, specific goal, start working towards it. You know where you're going. But if your only goal is, "I'm going to write a thesis," you will feel overwhelmed. There's no way you will write a thesis today. There are a lot of things—chunks—that you can do today, however, that will get you closer to having your thesis written.

Let me give you an example based on the way theses were written in my program.

Our thesis proposal had four chapters. There was the literature review, the rationale and hypotheses, the methods, and the proposed analyses and potential limitations. The typical thesis proposal document was somewhere between

20 and 40 pages of text, plus references, appendices, and so forth.

Before one of my advisees started writing their literature review, I made sure we both knew at a "bullet-point" level what was going to go in each of the other chapters. What were the hypotheses, how did they intend to conduct the study, and how did they foresee analyzing the data? It didn't have to all be thoroughly described, but we needed to know what we were building toward.

(I keep saying "we" because a thesis is a collaborative document. You are designing and executing it, but you have your chair/advisor, and that person is invested in you and your success. We want you to do well! If you can't describe your study in sufficient detail that your chair can visualize what your hypotheses, methodology, and analytic strategy are like, you aren't ready to write.)

So there's a four-part breakdown to start with, but the lit review typically has anywhere from three to five major sections, and each of those major sections has sub-sections, and you have to figure out which sources need to be referenced in which of the major sections and sub-sections, and if this sounds like I'm telling you that it's all easier when you have an outline, that's because IT'S ALL EASIER WHEN YOU HAVE AN OUTLINE.

You don't sit down one day and just say, "I'm going to write my lit review, now." Not if you want to remain sane. You pick a chunk and say, "I'm going to write at least three paragraphs on [favorite concept]. I'm going to make sure to use those five articles sitting right there as part of my writing." Then you do it. When you're done, you set a new goal. Maybe you take a break before setting the new goal, maybe you take a break after setting the new goal. Breaks matter.

Figuring out what comes next matters, but remember that you don't have to do it all right now.

Know what you're going to work on before you commit to the keyboard. Know what you hope to accomplish, in any given writing session. Going in with the goal to draft a specific chunk of the document makes it much more likely that you will come away from the writing process having accomplished something.

And if, for whatever reason, that chunk is not ready to be written by your brain, pick another. As you'll see in a bit, in my experience when you get stuck on what you want to write about, it's often because there's something else that you **need** to write about. You just haven't realized it yet.

Breaking things up into chunks allows you to see your progress. That is one of the most important things you can do for yourself, while working on your thesis—or any other large project.

Connections, Coherence, and Flow

In your head, everything makes sense. As you write, you know what you mean. But think about what I've said, so far, in terms of approaching the writing process. You will write a chunk at a time. You may be a little nonlinear in your approach to writing, but for me it's easiest to write one section/chunk, then move on to the next.

At some point, the "chunks" you've created will need to be glued together. One of your key tasks, as you revise, will be to make the document feel like a consistent, integrated, argument.

Remember: you are arguing your position and the entire

document needs to consistently and coherently build that argument. A lot of the argument-building happens in the lit review chapter, then culminates in the presentation of the hypotheses (if you have those in your discipline) or thesis statement. Whatever kind of thesis you write, though, you will likely have to review relevant literature. If you don't have to do any kind of literature reviewing, you probably stopped reading this book long, long ago.

The topics within the literature review have to flow from one to the next, so be aware of transitions. As you wrap up one section, you ought to provide a short summary that concludes with a statement such as, "With the research on [iggly-boo] reviewed, it makes sense to next turn our attention to [farfel], in order to understand [something about something important and why farfel makes sense in this context]." Draw a map for your reader as you go. At every step, make the reader comfortable following your logic and presentation. Then, when you get to the hypotheses or the core of your argument, take a few short paragraphs to summarize the key points from the literature review and present your hypotheses.

Everything in your document should align. Reviewing the literature and then presenting totally logical/reasonable hypotheses only works if you then describe a methodology that can test what you've set up. In early drafts of Methods chapters, I've seen students propose methodologies that not only didn't test their research hypotheses, they re-defined key concepts they discussed from the beginning of the document!

The exclamation point makes that seem like it's a bigger deal than it is, probably. Remember, for most of you this is the first thesis you've written. You are, in some respects, guessing at the best way to approach your central question.

You need to be talking with your chair. Lay out what you think is reasonable, make sure that's going to align with everything you've argued so far, and move forward. If you end up with a disconnect between hypotheses and methods, don't beat yourself up. Just figure out (with your chair, your fellow students—really, anyone who will listen to you and help you problem-solve) how to fix it. Once you identify a problem, you can fix that problem.

Then make sure that, if you're doing any kind of analyses (quantitative or qualitative), you know how to accurately test your hypotheses. Depending on how much training in statistics or design you have, this might be a challenge. Just come at it logically; figure out what your hypotheses are saying you expect to be the case, look at the variables you're testing and how they're measured, and determine the best statistical approach.

In other words, your lit review ought to logically lead the reader to your hypotheses, and your hypotheses ought to be testable with the methodology you have chosen and with the statistical techniques you describe in your proposed analyses. *Everything has to align.* This alignment is one of the major things that helps to make a thesis proposal in the social sciences approvable by your committee. Not the only thing, by far—but if any of those elements are mis-aligned, you are setting yourself up for trouble later.

A lot of the work of making connections will happen in the second and subsequent drafts. Just bear in mind that drawing that "map" for your reader, and helping your reader follow the map from the start of the document to its conclusion, is a major part of your job as a writer. If the story (there it is again, that word...) falls apart, readers will find something else to do.

Don't let them.

Use Your Chair!

You're probably expecting a joke about not writing on the floor. Sorry. Not happening. Chalk this up as yet another of the little disappointments in the thesis-writing process.

In another section, I will tell you to take control of your writing. This is, after all, your project. You write by yourself, but you don't operate in a vacuum. You will write, and you will give material to your chair, and you will get feedback. Some of the feedback will be positive and some of it will not, but it is all (hopefully) meant to be constructive.

Here's the thing with chairs: We want you to do well. You will be proposing and defending your thesis to our peers, and if you look bad, we look bad. We want you to look good.

That doesn't mean we'll write your thesis for you. It means that when you get feedback from us, even if it's not what you want to hear, it's meant to help improve your document. Writing advice, organizational advice, formatting advice, whatever—your chair is motivated to help you.

So, some of our motivation is kindness, and some of it is ego. Some of it is pretty functional, though. Your chair is an academic, and academics need to keep publishing. If you do well with your thesis and publish it, your chair may (I would say "should") get co-author credit. Depending on the university where you're studying, that may either be a big deal, or just a deal. But another publication never hurts faculty members.

If you're at all uncertain about the publishing norms for theses, or whether faculty in your program are generally co-authors on publications and presentations deriving from theses they've chaired, ask your fellow grad students and, to be honest, your chair. Because you will be getting feedback and guidance at every stage from your chair, to me it's 100% appropriate to give that person co-author credit. It's your document, but if they have read every section multiple times and contributed to the shaping of the thesis and its arguments in substantive ways, that satisfies just about any standard for "Should this person be a co-author?" that I can think of. That being said, the level of independence and rigor may differ between theses and dissertations in your program, so while I stand behind the "100%" statement for theses, dissertations may require more conversations and discernment around co-authorship.

Your chair is one of many resources you have at your disposal, and the resource best positioned and motivated to be a huge help. Use them to work through complex or painful parts of the document. Remember that your chair has been through this process a few times before, and ultimately has your best interests at heart. That makes it easier, when the inevitable bad feedback comes. Now, a few other things to remember, to help your chair help you.

Aesthetics matter. If you present an ugly document, your chair's focus will be on why it's not easier to read. If you have five different sets of tracked changes highlighted in their own colors, with some deleted text still there with a red strike-through, even your chair (who has seen the document before) will have a hard time with it. Present something where aesthetics don't detract from content.

Spellcheck and grammar check are your friends. At least early on, having spellcheck and grammar check turned on as you type can be helpful. They can also be a distraction, though. I never work with them on, because as far as I'm concerned, Word is often full of crap when it comes to grammar. And sometimes, sentence fragments are fine. But if you're not confident about your writing or spelling ability, make sure to use spellcheck and grammar check before you send anything to your chair. Some AI grammar-check software is fine, but be careful not to slavishly accept every suggestion from Word, or any other app. They're good with rules (for the most part), but trash with nuance.

Tracked changes aren't just for convenience. If you're getting an electronic document back with all sorts of markup and changes included, it's for a reason. (If you're getting a hard copy, skip the rest of this section.) You may be tempted to just accept all the tracked changes in a document at once, for simplicity's sake. If your chair is tracking changes, though, it's because they want you to actually SEE the changes, and think about why they were necessary. Same principle as above, but a different reason. If you just accept all the changes blindly, you won't be able to tell what text got changed and what didn't, and that defeats the purpose of tracking changes. If we wanted you to just change things to exactly how we think they ought to be without a second thought, we wouldn't turn on "track changes." We'd just change stuff.

Managing edits on the drafts you're sent is an active experience, and part of the learning process. Does it feel better to just accept all of the changes at once? Does it save you time?

Maybe it makes you feel better; maybe not. But it only saves you time in the short term. If you don't know why something got changed, odds are, you're going to make the same mistake again. Then you'll have more changes to accept, and maybe a meeting with your chair where you have to explain why you keep making the same errors, over and over.

You really don't want to have that meeting.

∾

Expect Revisions. Lots of Revisions.

I have a one-page document that I print out and hand to anyone who says, "Morrie, I'd like you to chair my thesis." It's creatively titled, "Working with Morrie," and describes my typical process for working with a thesis advisee. There are lots of caveats, since no two students are the same, and I modify my process based on the student's preferred mode of writing, but I feel like it's important to establish my norms and expectations up front.

"Morrie, that paragraph goes in another section."

Thanks for the revision note, but nope. It really doesn't. You see, kind reader, that one-page document includes a line that sometimes makes students' eyes threaten to pop out of their heads. In describing the lit review, I tell them that the number of drafts before the lit review is finalized varies across students, but that it's generally somewhere between three and thirty.

The idea that they could have to revise something three whole times is foreign to most students. Thirty? What kind of hell do I plan to inflict upon them, anyway?

Reality time: Very few students keep it anywhere near three drafts of the lit review. Part of that, admittedly, is that I refuse to read the entire lit review at once. We'll work on a section at a time. Most individual sections take more than three drafts to finalize, and then figuring out how to make sure all of the sections flow together takes some time, and once all the pieces are written, the order that we thought made sense no longer made sense—and so it goes.

I've had a few students get lit reviews done in a small number of drafts, but those students came in as kind of exceptional writers, and had done research writing in the past. Everyone revises, though. If it's your first time, you will be revising a lot.

Most of writing, my dad liked to tell me when I was in high school, is re-writing. He wasn't wrong. (Obligatory dad-style edit: "Saying 'He was right' is preferable, to avoid the double-negative." Again—not wrong...) The first draft is a necessary evil, which some writers call "word-vomit." It feels so good to get it out of our system that it takes some distance to realize just how unpleasant it really is. (Not every metaphor works well. This is also something you can fix in revision, or point out in revision so you can pretend you meant to write it that way the first time. In a parenthetical. Like this one.)

Early drafts need to focus on the argument. Are you making your points clearly? Did you summarize existing material in a way that supports what you want to say? Try to resist doing too much cleaning and line-editing right now. There's time for that later. If the arguments don't work, doing a bunch of word-changes and punctuation-fixes will be wasted, because you may cut or re-write entire paragraphs that you've prematurely spent time fine-tuning.

As you look at your early drafts, here are some questions to consider:

1. What is this section supposed to accomplish, and is it the right section to follow the one before?

2. How do we go from this section to the next one? Have all of the key terms been adequately defined?

3. Does this paragraph make the point I want it to make, and is it the right point to be making at this stage in the document?

You have to worry about flow and argument development all the way down to the level of the sentence. It's not always going to be fun, and it's not always going to be pretty, but it needs to happen. When things are where they need to be, then it's time to get into the micro-editing.

$$\sim$$

Dealing With Negative Feedback

At some point, you will send your chair a draft that you're proud of, then get feedback that makes you feel about two inches tall.

I think of this as the "Got Three A's!" syndrome. (Side note: I hate myself for having an apostrophe to pluralize the grade "A" in this paragraph. Apostrophes aren't used to pluralize. But "Got Three As!" makes it looks like there ought to be a follow-up question of "Three As What?" So I'm leaving the grammatically-incorrect apostrophe because to me, it's clearer than the correct punctuation.) There was a commercial when I was younger that involved a kid running home, all excited, bursting through the door and, as it swung shut behind him, shouting, "I got three A's!" Huge grin, really proud of himself. And the response, from the off-camera adult? "Don't slam the door!"

The kid's face falls. Cue sad music. Thirty years later, remembering this commercial still kicks me in my gut.

You're unlikely to get a "Don't slam the door!" moment from your chair, but it's possible. What you will get is feedback that says something like the following.

"This isn't consistent with what we talked about last time. I found the new sections confusing."

"The writing is uneven, and the argument kind of gets lost in the citations. What were you going for?"

"I was hoping for a bigger step forward, with this draft."

"This isn't some of your better work."

You get the idea. You open a document to see the feedback on something you're proud of, and instead of praise you get an ego-bruising, or what my clinical colleagues might call a "narcissistic injury." You worked hard on something, and the hard work isn't recognized.

Bad news: Hard work doesn't always get recognized.

Worse news: This is not the last time your hard work will not only be un-recognized, it will be treated as mainly irrelevant. In life, people don't always communicate exactly what they expect of you, or if they do, they don't tell you how to deliver it. Given that your chair is a person, they will sometimes do that. Not in what's intended to be a mean way —but sometimes, your chair will have read your draft after reading two or three other drafts, and various emails and papers and memos and things that not only were not written well, may have put them in a bad mood. And being human, that bad mood will sometimes translate into how feedback gets provided.

We don't set out to make students unhappy. I promise. It just happens, sometimes.

The thing you have to remember is that a chair who gets really frustrated isn't just frustrated with you; they're also frustrated with themselves.

We like to think we're pretty good at mentoring students. When we mentor a student, and they don't succeed, we may take that as a personal failing—another narcissistic injury, if you will. So sometimes, the frustration you perceive is the chair's frustration with themselves as much as it is with you.

Remember: Unless your chair tells you, "This is clearly not the right field FOR YOU. YOU ought to drop out of the program," the feedback is NOT ABOUT YOU. It's about your document. You are not your document. You wrote down some words in a particular order, and for one reason or another, those words in that order didn't work for your chair. So long as you're not being grabbed by the ear and dragged out to the curb, your chair has every expectation that whatever is wrong with the document, YOU can fix it.

Room to grow. Feedback is hard to give and hard to get, especially when it's critical. Unless your chair is a Grade-A jerk, they don't enjoy beating your ego. Students who feel beaten are much less likely to take risks and try something new, and much more likely to just do what feels "safe"—which often translates to, "Write something that sounds as much like my chair as possible, but is somehow even more boring."

Avoid that temptation. Yes, some amount of sounding like your chair (or anyone who edits your work heavily) is inevitable. But that's not the purpose of feedback. It's to get you to push yourself. To grow. That's what graduate school is about, and it's one of the ways it differs from a lot of undergraduate experiences. In undergraduate classes, the instructors may only interact with you for fifteen weeks. If you're lucky, you may write a paper and give a presentation, and the instructor will give you grades based on a (slightly) diverse set of abilities. If you're less lucky, you will take some multiple choice tests, and receive grades based on a much narrower set of abilities.

You've already figured out that grad school is a different universe from undergrad. In two to five years, your chair and the other faculty expect to see you grow into someone who can be a colleague. You will get pushed, and they will have high expectations of you, and that is exactly what you need if you're going to succeed in your field.

Feedback—critical or not—is not an indictment of you

as a person, nor is it a critique of your capacity. It is an opportunity for you to grow.

Dust off, dammit. Here is my process for receiving critical feedback: In phase one, I swear a lot, tell my wife or my dogs or anyone who will listen that the other person (chair, editor, reviewer, whatever) has no freaking idea what they're talking about. They just don't get it. In phase two, I calm down and walk away from the document for a few hours. If I'm really mad, I'll go for an actual physical walk in the park. If I'm really, REALLY mad, I'll take my dog, because she loves walks and is a font of joy and it's really hard to stay mad while following a tail that never stops wagging.

I mean, I'm still ruminating on the fact that someone had the audacity not to see the brilliance of what I wrote, but I'm not doing it where I'm in any danger of sending an angry email or text message. I'm also attending to my own mental health.

And my dog's.

In phase three, I try to put myself in the other person's position. What is it that they saw, or didn't see, that led to the feedback? Might there be something I hadn't considered? This perspective-adoption is vital, not just for the thesis, but for life. You will usually know exactly what you mean when you communicate an idea to another person. The fact that you know what you mean is no guarantee that they will, though, so when communication that originated with you breaks down, you can either (a) get angry at the person for being such an imbecile that they can't understand what you mean or (b) figure out how to help them understand. Helping the reader understand what you want to communicate is THE ENTIRE POINT OF WRITING.

This leads to phase four, wherein I figure out whether

the critique has merit (it often does, but not always) and how I can best address it.

It's fine and normal to get angry at critical feedback. But if you stop there, you've missed the point. Get angry. You have my permission. ("Gee, thanks...") Then figure out where the disconnect is, between you and your reader, and what can be done about it.

The critic is not always right. You do not always have to change what you are doing to satisfy the critic. But if you are not going to change something based on reasonable criticism, you need to be able to articulate why.

Among possible critics, your chair will be right more often than not. Pick your battles with your chair very, very carefully. I would advise always trying to walk through the four-phase process when you get unexpected feedback on a draft.

I. Get pissed.

II. Get calm.

III. Get perspective.

IV. Get a solution.

～

Give Yourself Permission to be Terrible

First drafts are, in general, trash. They are replete with terrible ideas, executed badly.

This comes as a horrific surprise to students who have written papers at the last minute for most of their lives and managed to get good grades (usually in the A/B range), due in part to high native ability and in part to papers being farmed out to over-worked, under-paid, teaching assistants.

We're not talking about the teaching assistants, though,

or the fact that your instructors may have never given you really hard critical feedback and forced you to re-write anything. We're talking about the fact that first drafts—yours, mine, Mark Twain's, William Faulkner's—suck. Part of the writing process is recognizing that you will inevitably write something that sucks, and that writing something that sucks is not the end of the world.

In fact, it's part of the—wait for it ...

...keep waiting ...

Part of the process.

Do not be afraid of writing something bad. If you're afraid of writing something bad, you will only write things that are safe. If you only write safe things, you will only write boring things. You will be the literary and scholarly equivalent of the guy in the Prius who cruises along in the middle lane at one mile per hour over the speed limit, because the middle lane is the safest based on the lack of merging traffic and the fact that the lunatics drive in the outer lane. If you've been behind me—er, I mean, that hypothetical guy—you know that there's nothing interesting about what he's doing. This is a calculated way of proceeding that minimizes risk while ignoring the experience of everyone around him. Sometimes acceptable for driving, not so much for writing.

You have something to say—say it! Put yourself out there! You will make mistakes, but guess what? That's why you have a chair. That's why you have a committee. If you make a mistake, someone will tell you about it, and you'll have a chance to fix it.

Learn from failure. Many of us seem to believe that if we fail, it diminishes our worth as a human being. The problem is, that notion is fundamentally full of crap, and ignores empirical literature that says we learn quite a bit from failure (e.g., Boss & Sims, 2008). Making mistakes widens our view of what we're trying to learn while increasing our ability to deal with setbacks. Who is going to be more resilient out in the "real world" when a mistake gets made—the person who has made plenty of mistakes and learned how to recover, or the person who has very carefully avoided any situation that might lead to looking bad, let alone failing?

Writing is not about avoiding mistakes. Not writing that has any hope of being interesting, at least. You need to give yourself permission to be terrible. Your first draft will suck, but terrible first drafts can become reasonable second drafts, and solid third drafts, and as you continue revising you will start to see just how much better your writing and your arguments become.

Revision is just stupidly important. Lots more on that to come. Don't get down on yourself if you don't get it right on the first (or the fifth) try. Because, among other things...

Writing is a skill. Skills require development. Development takes time and effort. I was lucky. When I was a junior in high school, I had to write a three-page paper every week for my English class. I wrote other papers for other classes, too. In college, I didn't write as many papers per unit time as I did during that one year in high school, but because I enrolled in an Honors College, I wrote a lot.

All that writing helped me develop facility with words. I have no idea how many millions of words I've written, when you consider all of the modes of writing in which I have engaged over the course of the past forty-ish years.

I'm not assuming you have that much practice, nor am I saying you need that much practice in order to write your thesis. What you need is the willingness to work to get better. You need to sit down and write, then listen to feedback, then revise what you've written to make it better. That's how you develop the skill of writing.

Creating a thesis is a process. Focus on the process of writing, not the product. The only thing you can control is what you are doing right now. What you've already done is already done. The defense meeting and all of that—it's in the future. Focus on what you are doing right now and stay aware of the process you've undertaken. If you focus on the process, the product will take care of itself.

Notes on Editing and Revisions

As I moved into the final stages of this book, I found myself faced with a yummy irony. My "notes on editing and revisions" was the single longest section of the book. By, like, a lot. It clocked in at around 4400 words. If you figure that a typed page is somewhere in the 250-300 word range, that means I had 14-22 manuscript pages written about editing.

My material on editing needed editing.

I've cut it back dramatically, but most of the material I've taken out—the full versions of each of the sections on word choice, sentence editing, and paragraph editing and revision —will be available as bonus content on my website (https://www.morriemullins.com/bonus). Editing and revisions are vital, but dumping that much into the middle of the book just felt excessive.

For some students, the first time they get detailed feedback on a paper may be their first paper in graduate school, or a first draft of a thesis. If you are in that position—if you have never had anyone read something you've written and give you detailed feedback—I would strongly recommend taking the first draft of what you write for your thesis to your school's writing lab or a more senior grad student before sending it to your chair. I suppose it's okay if you don't have other good options and your first feedback comes from your thesis chair. Just bear in mind that the first round of feedback may be traumatic. You got into grad school. You're smart. You're capable. You can do this. Then you get back a draft that either has a ton of red ink on it (if you've got an old-school chair, who likes to read and mark up hard copies) or a margin full of comments and tracked changes. Like I've said elsewhere, that can feel pretty rough.

In this section, I'll talk about a few different ways you can focus on editing and revising. Maybe a better way to say it is "different levels," since when you write you are building words into sentences, sentences into paragraphs, paragraphs into sections, and sections into the full document. I'm going to focus on those first three levels—words, sentences, and paragraphs—because until you get those down, there's no way your writing will be as clear as it can get. Plus, the structure of the document differs from program to program, making it hard to give general advice on documents as a whole.

Choosing the right words. As you work on revising your work, try to make the language invisible. Make the words right. Your reader doesn't, by and large, care about whether you can use a sequence of five-syllable words that nobody has put in the same sentence since the mid-19th century. Your reader wants to hear what you have to say.

When you're writing (and this is a generic "you," which includes me!), you should be as precise as possible. The tendency, when we're trying to be precise, is to keep using precise words or phrases that are important to our point. This may lead to repetition of key words or phrases; if they're the best possible words or phrases, that's usually not a big deal. If it starts to feel repetitive, though, look at how you can streamline things.

There will be a lot of words you write that you just don't need. I'd estimate somewhere between 15% and 25% of them. You may not cut that many words, and that's fine. I think Stephen King's second-hand guidance in *On Writing* was something like, "Second draft equals first draft minus 10%."

Does that sound like the worst thing ever? That you will sit down, write ten pages, and only keep nine of them?

If so, I'd like to ask you—with all the kindness in my heart—to get over it. To maximize readability, you need to find irrelevant words and kill them. Kill them with fire.

The first type of irrelevant word that I'll pick on is the **redundancy**. Some are obvious (such as the infamous "Department of Redundancy Department"). Others come from including multiple words that convey the same basic information in a sentence.

For example: "The new corporate policy highlighted the company's own values."

That's a very first-draft sentence, and there's nothing wrong with it—in a first draft. Remember, early on, you're just trying to get ideas down on paper. And if you wrote this sentence, you might look at it and think, "Yes, that says exactly what I mean," and leave it alone.

The problem with the sentence is that if a company implements a policy to highlight its values, you don't need the word "own" in the sentence. If the sentence said "...the company's values," you have exactly the same information about whose values are being highlighted. In fact, you could go a step further and argue that the "corporate... company's" construction is also redundant, and that you really ought to remove "corporate" from the sentence as well, leaving "The new policy highlighted the company's values."

You need to look critically at all the words in the sentence, and make sure you haven't included words whose meaning is adequately carried by other words or phrases.

Redundant words are one thing to watch out for. We also have words that writers will fight over, when it comes to editing: adjectives and adverbs.

I won't say to never use an adjective or adverb. What kind of hypocrite would that make me? Pick a paragraph—yours or mine—that's more than three words long and do a count. How many adjectives (words that modify nouns or pronouns) and adverbs (words that modify adjectives, verbs, and other adverbs) are there? I mean, in the phrase "redundant words," the word "redundant" is an adjective, and important. Remove it, and the meaning of the sentence changes! And then you've got "carefully-constructed arguments," where you could remove "carefully-constructed" and still have the sentence make sense, but lose the additional meaning (and emphasis) "carefully-constructed" conveys.

One of the things I tell my students—a lot—is that they need to be sparing in their use of adjectives and adverbs. These "emphasis words" draw attention. If you use emphasis words for everything, it's like SHOUTING YOUR ENTIRE PAPER. Well-placed adjectives and adverbs can be powerful, and contribute to your argument. But having them all over the place can make your paper sound overblown and self-important.

Look carefully [intentional adverb!] at each word you write. Not as you write it—you'll never finish, then—but once you're editing, be brutal. If you can read the sentence without a word and lose none of the meaning, delete the word. You will never miss it.

"More words" does not equal "better" or "sounds smarter." You don't need a thesis with the most words. You need a thesis with the best words to communicate exactly what you want to say.

Sentence editing. You can write simple sentences. You can also write long, drawn-out, compound-complex sentences with tons of independent and dependent clauses, proper punctuation, a multitude of valuable points (some of them in the main body of the sentence, others potentially buried in parentheticals like this one), and have them be perfectly fine, and correct, and complete.

The more you cram into a sentence, though, the easier it is for your point (and your reader!) to get lost. The goal of the thesis, in most disciplines, is not to impress the reader with brilliant wordsmithing. It is to communicate your ideas and perspective. The more clearly you write and present your sentences, the easier it is for the reader to stay with you.

You should, in general, strive for simplicity of structure. Your ideas may be complex. Your sentences do not have to be. You want readers, to the extent they struggle with anything, to struggle with your ideas, to confront your arguments and critically examine them.

A note that I found myself giving a lot of students during their first semester of graduate school is that the reader will naturally breathe with the rhythm of your writing. Punctuation helps, to some extent. A comma is (sometimes) a place where a reader will naturally take a breath. But the most natural place for a reader to pause and breathe is at the end of a sentence.

This means a couple of things. First, when the sentence

ends, you should expect that the reader may pause and reflect on what you just said. Second, if you've got a particularly long sentence, the reader may have rushed to get to the end. A sentence that drags on for three or four lines is one that, if the reader is unconsciously pacing their reading to the rhythm of the writing, will lead that reader to start skimming in order to get to the magical full-stop where a breath is once again "allowed."

You don't want your readers to skim. You don't want to give them a reason to speed up and skip words. You want readers to read every word and pay attention to every idea. Otherwise, what was the point of writing the thesis?

A final thing that needs attention, at the level of the sentence, is whether the sentence is a re-statement of something you already said. Young writers in particular sometimes doubt their ability to communicate complex ideas. When you find yourself typing a sentence that starts, "In other words" or "That is," it's probably a sign you aren't sure you did it right the first time.

There's nothing wrong with that. If you think you didn't get the ideas across the first time, write your "In other words..." But when you go back through and edit your document, focus on those sentences. Do you need them, or have you created sentence-level redundancy? If there's sentence-level redundancy, you need to cut either the original or the "In other words" version. Often, the "In other words" will be what you keep; there's a reason you felt a need to re-state the original, after all.

Sometimes, though, repetition is not just appropriate, it's necessary. Repeating ideas or phrases is a powerful way to really hammer a point home. A little repetition goes a long way.

A little repetition goes a long way.

But a lot of repetition makes you sound like you're just trying to stretch your argument over more page-space.

A little repetition? It goes a long way.

Paragraph editing (or, "What the hell are paragraphs, anyway?") A few years ago, my university brought in a speaker to talk about mentoring student writing. The speaker's name was Dawn Skorczewski, and she had a lot of interesting things to say. The most important (or at least, the one that I still parrot to my students from time to time) had to do with paragraphs.

A paragraph, she said, is a unit of information. I think that's a great way to consider them, so I've continued to teach the idea. The phrase "unit of information" conveys a clear purpose: A paragraph should communicate something specific.

Now, that "something specific" can be narrow, or quite broad. You just need to make sure that your paragraphs aren't trying to do too much. You want to pick a single idea, or study, or concept, to focus on, and focus on it for that paragraph. If there are multiple facets to that idea, or study, or concept, you may need to have a paragraph for each facet. The busier a paragraph gets, the harder it is for the reader to understand your point.

Just like the reader will tend to breathe with the flow of your writing, so too will the reader pause at the end of a paragraph to mentally "take stock" of what you've just said. If you can't look at a paragraph and say, "This is specifically what the paragraph was about," you need to revise it. If you look at a paragraph and see that it shifts topics multiple times, that's probably a sign that you were doing an information-dump as you wrote, and that you need to figure out (a) what points you were trying to make, and (b) how to present those points in a series of paragraphs.

Mix up the length of your paragraphs. If your document is a consistent series of six- to seven-line paragraphs, it's going to read oddly. Remember that for a lot of the population, reading is a visual activity, but the principles here apply when reading is done by touch, or when a text is read aloud either as an audiobook or using screen-reading software.

A document with a large number of same-sized "blocks of text" may not affect the reader's conscious judgment of the quality of the text, but it will have an impact on the reader's perception on other levels. Not every point can be made in three sentences—but some can. Others require eight, ten, maybe even twelve or more sentences. With each paragraph, you ought to be searching for the right length to make the point that paragraph is designed to make.

Short paragraphs are fine.

Longer paragraphs are also fine.

When you're writing your first draft, write what you need to write and don't worry too much about paragraph length. It's all got to get out of your head. When you go back and edit, though, be very critical about the paragraphs. Do they serve their purpose, as units of information? Does the structure and order of the paragraphs make sense and contribute to your arguments? When readers finish each paragraph, will they know the take-away?

Don't be afraid to "hand-hold" the reader some. If you think the point you're making isn't clear, just come right out and say it. It's better to add a sentence at the end of a paragraph to draw everything together than it is to leave your reader wondering, "What the hell was all that about, anyway?"

Revising is a lot of work, but it feels good to look back at a document you've worked hard on and know that you've made it even better than it was to start.

~

When to Revise

There are writers—not just students, though the affliction hits students particularly hard sometimes—who write something, then go back to it, re-read it, hate it, scrap it, and start over. They look at what they've done, say, "This is crap!" and get discouraged.

C'mon, now. Of course it's crap—it's a first draft. We've been over that! Get through the draft, then let it sit a while before you start editing.

I like to put a manuscript aside for anywhere from a few days to a couple of months before I start editing. That lets me come back to it with fresh eyes. An extended break may or may not be possible, depending on your timeline.

My strong recommendation is to get a full first draft of the section you're working on before you start revising it. Now, the meaning of "section" may vary. A section might be eight pages of lit review, or it might be five paragraphs on a single topic. When you're able to look at a piece of what you've done and see a beginning, a middle, and an end, you've got a section. Easy as that.

Make yourself get through the whole section before you really start going back and asking yourself questions about it. When the time comes, though, here are some section-level questions you should ask, in (relative) order of importance:

What is this about?

Does it follow logically from what came before?

Does it create an expectation for the reader of what ought to come next?

Do all the pieces make sense? That is, do the paragraphs flow together well?

Is there any nit-picky crap that I screwed up the first time around? Grammar, punctuation, formatting, or whatever?

Do a broad read first. Think about how what you've written "fits." Don't worry about the minutiae (unless you've got that form of authorial OCD that makes it impossible for you to focus on big-picture issues when there are little details shouting for your attention, in which case by all means—fix those, so that you're able to deal with the rest of it!). Think of the section as a piece of a puzzle; as you're trying to fit that piece into the rest of the puzzle, you're looking at the edges, and how it can interlock with every-thing else. Being able to pull back and kind of see the section you're working on from above is difficult, but important.

The great part of this puzzle is that you can re-shape the edges as you go, to make sure all the pieces fit together. When you write a first draft, you make all the pieces. When you revise, you hack at them until they fit together and create the narrative of your document.

Anyway, try not to revise any section immediately after you finish drafting it. You only just chose those words, so unless they're glaringly wrong, OF COURSE they're going to seem fine. With a few days to separate you from the text, you'll be better equipped to be a good critic.

Review old drafts before starting to write or edit a new section. Go back and look at the comments on old drafts. If you had the same comment come up more than once, it's something to watch. If you had a comment from your chair about something specific, and you continue making the same mistake that elicited the comment, you're going to eventually make your chair cranky. Giving the same feedback over and over is a waste of time, and makes it feel as if we're not being listened to. It takes time to review a draft, and your chair puts a lot of effort into it. Try to avoid making the same mistake in multiple drafts.

Just because a section is "done" doesn't mean it won't get changed. Really, there's no such thing as "done" until you send your document to your committee. Even then, you'll go back through, re-read, and find things that you missed. Little typos. Or big ones. Paragraphs that could be re-arranged. Tables that don't have decimal points quite lined up. Mainly annoying little crap, but sometimes big, embarrassing crap.

That's okay. Remember: It's a process.

~

Feeling Blocked?

I'm not much of a believer in writer's block. It's not that I don't think it can happen; I just don't view it as a meaningful impediment to getting work done. You might not get the work done that you *wanted* to get done, but you can still get work done, even when you find yourself staring at a blank screen while your anxiety level skyrockets and your body starts threatening to collapse into a puddle of fear-flavored protoplasm.

There will be days when the words don't come. When that happens, see if you can figure out why.

In my experience, what we think about as writer's block doesn't come from having nothing to say; it comes from having too much to say. You may be looking at the thesis as an entire document, rather than looking at the section you're trying to work on right now. Or you may be thinking about later sections, rather than the one that you're trying to write. Or there may be an element of your logic that isn't working for you, that keeps what you're trying to write from actually fitting with the remainder of the document. In other words, your brain is refusing to focus on the task that you think it ought to focus on, and is instead going in two, or ten, or a thousand other directions.

Let's take the main problems I laid out in the prior paragraph one at a time.

Thinking about the thesis as a whole. Reality: The thesis is a big document. It may be the biggest thing you've ever written, in terms of page and word counts. If you think about the thesis as a whole in the early stages of writing it, you can paralyze yourself. "I'm supposed to write something that is [40/60/100] pages long? With what kind of margins and what kind of font and how many references and what else that I have to do that I have no idea about?"

It gets overwhelming. This is why when you sit down to write you should never say, "I am now going to write my thesis." There may be people who sit down and just crank out a thesis. I am not one of those people. If I were, this would be a short and useless book, because I would just say, "Sit down and write a thesis" and be done with it.

You are also not one of those people. If you were, you would not be reading this book. You'd be off, writing yet another thesis, because that's how you kill time.

What you do, when you sit down to write, is you create a small piece of what will become your thesis. You write 2-5 paragraphs on a topic, summarizing key articles or elements of your argument, then you link it to what came before and what comes after in your document, then you look at what you need to write next.

Your thesis ends up as a fairly long document, but your actual writing sessions will involve generating anywhere from a few sentences to a few pages of new material.

If one chunk of new material isn't something you can write today, pick another chunk. There are lots of pieces you can work on. But if you focus on the thesis as a whole, paralyzing yourself into anxiety-induced inaction is easy.

It's also beat-able.

Having the wrong focus. The second case, where you're focusing on the wrong part of the paper, is another sign that you ought to be writing something else. Yes, you sat down intending to write about self-esteem today. But if your brain is stuck on bullying, write about bullying! (Assuming bullying and self-esteem are both part of your thesis, of course. If not, you may have other problems.) Let yourself write about whatever your brain needs you to write about.

Or is it logic? If the logic isn't working for you—if something about your argument isn't ringing true—step back and open a different document. Start writing about what it is that isn't quite working. Describe the intended logic, and what you have, and the gap between the ideal and the reality. In other words, write it out.

For me, this works best if I switch away from the keyboard and write it out longhand. I can type sentence after sentence, paragraph after paragraph, about a problem. Sometimes I'll get resolution. Other times, I won't.

But when I've gotten really stuck on the logic of an argument or the plot of a story or whatever, grabbing a notebook and writing out my thoughts by hand has almost always led to some kind of breakthrough. Maybe it's the slower, more deliberate thought involved in writing by hand; I'm honestly not sure why it works for me. I'm just glad that it does!

Keep writing. You may not write what you planned to write, but in almost every case, you will write what you need to write. Even if it doesn't always feel that way.

~

Things To Do When You're Blocked

Format your document. Formatting can be disruptive and intrusive and annoying. It can frustrate the hell out of you, especially if you leave it until the end of your writing process. The bad news about formatting is that it's brainless work.

The good news about formatting? It's brainless work! It has to get done, so whenever you have the time and inclination, you can work on it. Or your chair may give you format-related feedback that makes it obvious where you have to change things. I wouldn't count on that, though, since your chair wants to be focusing on non-format portions of your document, and some happily ignore formatting. I mean, I had a professor when I was an undergraduate whose philosophy on preparing manuscripts for publication was, "I don't care about the formatting; the editor's going to want to change all that anyway, so I'll just focus on the words."

I never found that to be a constructive way to approach writing. Formatting isn't everything—but it's also not nothing. A poorly-formatted document looks unprofessional. It tells the reader that you don't care about how you're presenting the information. If you don't care about how you're presenting the information, why should the reader care about the information itself?

Probably the most text-intrusive element of the formatting (that is, hardest to do after the writing is finished) is the in-text citations. If you do nothing else, make sure to familiarize yourself with how to properly cite your sources. Those citations cannot and should not wait for later drafts, because if you send something to your chair that doesn't include citations, you will end up having a very awkward (and hopefully unnecessary) conversation about what constitutes plagiarism.

There will be days when you can't find the right words to make the point you want to make, or days when you just don't have the energy to either work on new first draft material or edit existing material. On those days, formatting drudgery can save you. If nothing else is clicking and you want to make sure you get something accomplished, format your document.

Departmental format requirements. It gets complicated if you've got both a style guide (e.g., APA, MLA) and departmental guidelines for how to format your document. That's something our school does; we're a psychology program, so we require students to write in APA style, but we also have specific formatting guidelines for a thesis. These include non-APA margins, sections of the document that lack APA headers, different requirements for placement of specific elements of the document than what APA would tend to recommend—annoying crap, in other words, that requires you to both know APA style and know when to violate it.

You can view this as a waste of time, or you can view it as another way to get something necessary done when you are otherwise struggling.

It's a mindset thing, ultimately. You will have good days, and you will have less-good days. If you learn to use the less-good days to get the "grunt work" of the thesis done, I won't claim you'll make them good days... but you'll get something accomplished, and that will make them *better* days.

Then you can go to sleep knowing that you did, in fact, make forward progress on your thesis.

∾

Take Control of Your Writing

You have to remember—and this is both empowering and somewhat scary—that you are in charge of your progress. You can't and shouldn't count on anyone else to set goals or deadlines for you. You shouldn't expect anybody to nag you (and don't ask them to, because you'll just resent them for it). This is all about you.

Writing is a solitary activity. You sit down, and maybe you have a cat curled up beside you, or a dog at your feet, or a small dog in your lap, or a bird on your shoulder. But your cat, dog, bird, goldfish, hamster, llama, or other writing-room companion will not write a damned word.

That "solitary activity" paragraph may have created some anxiety. If so, let the anxiety go. No one has written what you're writing before. You're free to say whatever you want! Yes, you'll have to go back and edit it later on, but first drafts are full of potential and ideas. Your potential. Your ideas. You get to shape that potential and those ideas into something that reflects you, and your point of view.

"Morrie, you're making it worse!"

Am I? Then take a couple of minutes and breathe. You'll be okay. You can do this.

What you will find is, as you write, you will lose yourself in the act of writing. You will enter what Csikszentmihalyi

(2008) describes as a "flow" state, where the words seem to arise organically from you. Your task is not always just to get the words written down or typed out; sometimes, your task is to get out of the way of the words and let them come.

The thing that you always control is the mindset that enables or gets in the way of words moving from brain to screen. Recognize that you are the one in control of your mind, which means you are the one in control of your writing. Accept that whatever you are writing in the moment is exactly what you need to be writing. It may not be what you sat down to write, but it's what you're writing Right Now.

Practice self-compassion. Remember that all progress is good progress. When you have inevitable moments of frustration, understand that what's happening is normal: a process that can be overwhelming has, in fact, temporarily overwhelmed you.

Don't write yourself into a stomach ulcer or an anxiety attack. Write something, and if your mind tells you that you need to take a short break, do that. Just make sure you come back!

Taking control of your writing doesn't mean forcing yourself to do something you aren't ready to do. It means accepting that you are more than capable of completing the task in front of you.

Because you are.

∽

You Are (probably) Not a (good) Multi-Tasker

We live in a world where lots of things compete for our attention. People watch TV while checking their phones or playing games all the time. The research pretty consistently shows, though, that trying to do more than one thing at a time decreases performance on one or both things (Srna et al., 2018). We're also not as good at it as we think; Srna et al. (2018) found that in a survey of over 400 people, 93% said that they were able to "multitask as well as or better than the average person" (p. 1942). I trust that your understanding of statistics makes it clear that a good chunk of that 93% cannot possibly be correct, which means that a great many people over-estimate their ability to multi-task.

So, you know... close the browser. Turn off the TV. Put your phone in another room, or get your best friend to pass-word-lock it for the next hour. If you need music, turn on music, put on noise-canceling headphones, and get ready to write. Remove the temptations to multi-task.

A BIG-BIG caveat, though:

Everything I just wrote? That's the "neurotypical" advice. Having now offered it, it's important to recognize that every brain works differently.

I once mused in class about whether the amount of attention deficit disorder we're seeing diagnosed might reflect a step in the evolution of how human brains work. Like, maybe it's an adaptation to help us function better in a world that increasingly seems to require multi-tasking. Maybe all of my friends and colleagues and students (and wife!) with ADD are a step ahead of undiagnosed-me, in an evolutionary sense. I'm not a clinician or a cognitive psychologist, though, so that really is a "musing" that isn't informed by data. Still, it makes me wonder.

The early understanding of multi-tasking as being diffi-cult or impossible related to the finding/reality that we're limited capacity information processors (Kanfer & Acker-man, 1989). It also came from a place that assumed neurotypicality, with neurodiversity not recognized as having adaptive value (which I'm confident it does, for many people). Because of that, saying "people can't multi-task" as a blanket statement is hard to support. It usually (again, based on lots of research) leads to worse performance than focusing on a single task, but if your brain needs something secondary to help you focus, that's important to know.

Here's the take-away: People aren't good at doing two different things that require attention at the same time, and many people over-estimate their capacity to do so. The safer approach, at least to start, is to minimize distractions.

Don't Be Boring!

A lot of academic writing is boring. There. I said it. For whatever reason, there are people—many who get to call themselves "editors"—who think that if writing is interesting, it's Done Wrong.

That's fundamentally silly, though! Academic writing can, indeed SHOULD, be interesting! Engaging! Even...

...fun to read.

Maybe your thesis will be fun to read. Maybe not. But you can at least make it not-boring. In order to be not-boring, you must first understand what makes writing boring for readers. Once you understand that, you can do something about it.

Imagine that you're reading something you've written. You stare at the words and you yawn, despite it being the middle of the day. What you've got is fine, but it bores the life out of you.

Why?

Readers put down a book or article if nothing is happening. If we're talking fiction, the plot has bogged down or the characters are sitting and doing the literary equivalent of thumb-twiddling. There's no conflict.

We're not writing fiction. Well, not in the social and behavioral sciences. I guess that in some fields—no, you know what? If you're writing fiction, there are probably better resources than this book to build your skills. Find them!

Even though most of us aren't writing fiction, boredom can come from a very similar place; it's just that when we're talking about writing a lit review, "nothing is happening" means, "You aren't making a point. You're just sharing information."

A lit review isn't just about sharing information. It's about sharing information in a way that gets you to what your study is about. If you're bored, then your reader will be bored, and bored readers find something else to read. Or start finding reasons to critique what you've written. As I like to tell my students, do not give your reader reason to start critiquing; keep their attention.

Which means, to put it succinctly, make a damned point.

Every paragraph ought to make a point. If all you did in a paragraph is present information, you have provided zero value-added to your reader, and done nothing to enhance your own work.

Take this paragraph, for example:

"Mullins (2015) noted that engagement had to be thought of more broadly than might otherwise be the case. Most discussions of motivation focus on variables like attention and focus (Smith, Smith, & Jones, 2012). Moving beyond those kinds of cognitive characteristics pushes us to reconsider what we mean by 'engagement' and to work to create more excited and productive workers."

And? So what? Look at the verbs in the paragraph. We've got "noted," "focus," "moving," and "pushes." These are kind of wishy-washy, as verbs go. Oh, Mullins "noted" something? Bless his heart.

Whenever someone gives me a paper in which people repeatedly "note" things, I die a little inside. Authors rarely just "note" things that matter. They may "argue" or "assert" them, but "noting" is kind of rare. I mean, it implies that the information was stuck in a foot- or end-note and makes it sound unimportant. To "note" something is not to make a point—it's to offer an, "Oh, by the way..."

So, we ought to fix the verbs. What else?

The paragraph **needs a compelling point**. Not just any old point. Something that matters. There needs to be something that the reader can grab onto and say, "This—this is what is important."

"Mullins (2015) argued that typical ideas of engagement may be insufficient. Despite the importance of motivation to modern organizations (and we would find a citation to put here, because they are many), many of the common 'markers' of engagement are limited to cognitive variables such as attention and focus (Smith, Smith, & Jones, 2012). If we truly want to create engaged organizations, our field must move beyond narrow conceptualizations of 'engagement.' No amount of discussion of the importance of engagement can possibly matter, if we fail to consider not only what employees think, but also what they feel, and what they do."

The paragraph still has problems. It's over-written, I totally made up the source, and it contains more adverbs than I'd like—but it makes a point. It's twice the length of the first paragraph, but I'd suggest that it's less boring, because it's more than just an information-dump. It gives the author's perspective.

Things that work to get people's attention in other media don't work as well in most thesis or dissertation writing. Most research papers don't involve sex (in its non-demographic usage), blowing things up (with noteworthy exceptions from physics/chemistry/etc.), or random profanity.

So you're more limited in what you can do, to keep your reader's attention. Get creative! Then ask yourself, "What point am I making with all of this information? And have I made it?"

Remember that you are very close to your text. You inherently see the connections that you mean to make. So it takes a little distance, and a willingness to self-critique, to figure out when the connections aren't being made.

Having other people read it is also helpful.

∾

AI and You

It's difficult to poke your head into a LinkedIn thread giving advice about thesis writing without finding someone saying, "AI will make your thesis process so much easier!"

I mean... kinda? Maybe?

It depends on what you mean by "easier." There are things generative AI is good for, as I'm working to get this book finalized, and things that it's really not good for.

One thing I see more than I'd like is commenters saying, "This can take away the drudgery of summarizing articles!" Which I suppose is true. You can feed your AI pet of choice an article and tell it to summarize the article, and it will. I mean, GPT-era gen AI excels at parsing text. It can summarize what the article says in a way that's succinct and (usually) accurate.

That's not the same as understanding what an article means, though. ChatGPT, Deep Seek, and Google Gemini don't "understand" anything. They mathematically model the text and distill it down, if you ask them to summarize it.

"So Morrie, what you're saying is that they can summarize articles for my lit review?"

Sure. That's what I'm saying. If you want to write a paper like a high school sophomore, where you summarize the articles as written and add none of your insights, then yes. You can use generative AI to do that.

I mean, I wouldn't *recommend* it, since if you want to publish it after you're done, work co-written by AI may not end up able to be copyrighted.

Also, depending on your university or program's guidelines, you may be engaging in academic dishonesty.

Oh, and if summarizing articles is all you're doing as you "review literature" for your thesis, I would suggest—not particularly humbly, in this case, but also not in a way meant to be unkind—that you're Doing It Wrong. Because the purpose of reviewing literature is not simply to summarize what others have done. It is to both summarize *and integrate* existing work in a way that builds a case for your unique contribution.

Okay, time for a rant. I figure I get to do this every once in a while, but it's polite to offer a warning first. So, warning: rant incoming. Sub-warning: it's not the anti-AI rant you may be expecting.

One of the things generative AI highlights is a **significant and on-going failure in how we educate our students.** The failure is inherent somewhat in what we reward students for doing, but much more in what we punish students for doing.

There is a lot—and I mean, a LOT—of emphasis on

writing mechanics, in the modern US educational system. (If you're not in the US, read what comes next and consider the extent to which it applies to how you were taught writing.) By which I mean, you learn your nouns and your verbs, your pronouns and their antecedents, your adjectives and your adverbs. You learn the difference between a colon and a semi-colon, the myriad rules related to comma usage, when to put things in "quotation marks" (and when to put them in parentheses). You learn that you shouldn't start a sentence with a conjunction, or end it with a preposition, which means that you also learn about conjunctions and prepositions, and gerunds, and participles, and verb tenses, and paragraphs, and lots of other things that I may or may not have even bothered to talk about earlier in this part of the book.

Then, whenever you write something, you get graded based on whether you did all of the above correctly. And there are SO MANY rules, and SO MANY ways to get things wrong (because, let's face it—English is a messy language that is not at all intuitive, and has silly rules like "i before e, except after c," which get all sorts of caveats added on so that they're less "rules" than "stepped-up nursery rhymes"), that students are repeatedly bludgeoned with feedback about HOW they wrote, rather than WHAT they wrote.

AI appeals in part because writing is hard. It is. It's hard both cognitively (it takes effort!) and emotionally. When we write something, even for an assignment, we're putting part of ourselves on the page. We want to protect that part of ourselves. When so much time and energy spent on feedback goes into the "how" rather than the "what," the message students are likely to hear is that what they have to say doesn't matter, if they don't say it "correctly."

You need to follow most of the conventions of writing if

you're going to clearly communicate your message. As such, focusing on mechanics makes sense.

But when you've been getting feedback on comma-splices and incorrect pronoun-antecedent connections and the need to use (or not use) the Oxford comma for years, and a tool is put in front of you that can make all of that negative feedback go away? Your inclination is likely to be to use it.

The allure of generative AI is that it can help you create a clean product more quickly and easily. The problem, from a thesis perspective, is that even though it's the product that gets you the degree, it's the process that gets you the skills that will help you once you're out of school. Education should not be just about the product, and when done well, it isn't. The process—sometimes hard, sometimes frustrating, sometimes magical—is where the learning happens. It's where changes occur that give you the capacity to think differently, more broadly and richly, than a person who has not had the opportunity to get a graduate degree.

Graduate school, and the writing of a thesis or dissertation, is an opportunity to build skills that differentiate you from others, in terms of the contributions you can make to the workplace, and to society at large. Learning how to effectively use AI will likely be important to all of us, but it won't differentiate you from a significant chunk of the population. So learn to use it, but don't use it in a way that short-changes the building of key thinking and writing skills that will give you a real advantage for the rest of your life.

∼

Writing by Not-Writing

I talk a lot about writing in this book. Which makes sense—
it's a book about writing a thesis. But there is also something
to be said for not-writing, particularly in the context of my
earlier discussion of writer's block, and my notes on taking
control of your writing.

Although I gave a few examples of why writer's block
may manifest in the thesis-writing process, far and away the
most common that I've seen is students who just have too
much to say, who are trying to write the final document
rather than the next draft, and who let themselves get overwhelmed.

In such cases, the writer's mind has too much "noise."
It's a common thing; our brains are noisy, by virtue of
how much sensory input we have to cope with, and we've
probably made them even noisier over the past few years
as technology gives us more and more ways to gather
information. We compulsively multi-task, which is prob-
lematic because as I note elsewhere, we're generally not
great at it. If we think about too much, we focus on
nothing.

There's a great example of what I mean in *Zen and the
Art of Motorcycle Maintenance*. (Yes, it's a real book. Yes, it's an
amazing book.) The author, Robert Pirsig, talks about
teaching writing to a student struggling to find anything to
say. Pirsig progressively narrows the focus of the assignment
from writing about US history, to writing about the town
where they live, to writing about the main street in the town
where they live, to writing about one building on that street
—starting with the brick in the upper left corner of the
building.

It's only when he gives that last instruction—to start

with one brick—that the student becomes "un-stuck" and finds something to say.

Pirsig's take-away from this is different from mine, to some extent, but also not. "She was strangely unaware that she could look and see freshly for herself, as she wrote, without primary regard for what had been said before," he says. That's part of it, I think; we don't trust our own insights about the world and feel like we have to try to re-create what's already been done—a temptation that's particularly marked when reviewing literature.

But there's also the issue of scope. When you think about everything at once, your brain tries to write about everything at once. When you focus in on one thing—one brick—you let everything else go and can start writing.

If you find yourself with too much going on, with too many thoughts sprouting at once in the field of your mind, you need to stop writing. At least for a few minutes. Step back and examine what you're building. Find the one piece that you need to focus on, your "brick," and let the rest go.

This doesn't work if it's just a cognitive exercise. Or at least, it doesn't work for me. There needs to be something behavioral as well. Sometimes, in order to start writing, you have to stop writing.

Put the keyboard down. Turn away from your monitor, or your notebook, or whatever you're using to compose. Don't turn on the TV or grab your phone, just disengage so that you can get yourself ready to re-engage.

Start by closing your eyes and breathing.

Some people prefer to breathe in through the nose, out through the mouth.

If you've taken yoga classes, you may have been taught to only breathe through your nose.

It doesn't matter which way you do it. What you want to

do to calm your mind is focus on your breath. Count the breaths going in and out. Start by trying for three seconds in, three seconds out. Then go to four. Five. Six. Seven. Seven is a nice number, since by the time you're doing a seven-second inhale and a seven-second exhale, you're down close to four breaths a minute. "Normal" resting for an adult is anywhere from 12-20 breaths per minute, and the slower you breathe, the more you relax.

Focusing on your breath, and counting from one to seven, then back down from seven to one, gives you something to focus on that's not your thesis. Even a couple of minutes of letting yourself relax and breathe can go a long way toward starting to clear your mind.

This isn't a book about meditation, but I will say that what I just described is one form of/precursor to meditative practice. Mindfulness meditation in particular can be great to reduce stress and quiet a mind that's gotten too busy and noisy. Given how stressful and noisy graduate school can be, developing a mindfulness practice can be helpful—and as it happens, there was a paper published a while back about the benefits of mindfulness meditation to graduate students (Cabrera-Caban et al., 2016).

Sitting and staring at a screen when the words aren't coming doesn't reduce stress. It increases it. Giving yourself permission to stop, to step away, to gather your thoughts and to just breathe can really help.

It's important, though, that after you take that break you go back and start writing. It doesn't matter what. Write the first thing that comes to mind. Then let yourself meander toward the topic you'd planned on writing about. The first few sentences or paragraphs may be dreadful; if so, it's because your brain had a bunch of gunk clogging it up, and by giving yourself permission to not-write and relax for a little while, you loosened up the gunk. Once it's out of the way, you can get back to the writing that needs to happen.

Your Audience is the World

That sounds a little grandiose, doesn't it? "Your audience is the world."

Could I perhaps be a *little* more puffed-up and self-important? Maybe?

Let me try unpacking things a bit, then, starting from a pair of assumptions.

Assumption one: the work you are doing on your thesis will make a scholarly contribution to your field, and will (if successful) be read by other academics in your discipline.

Assumption two: the work you are doing has the potential to make a difference outside academia.

Much of the thesis mentorship you are likely to get, including some of what I've written, focuses on the first assumption. It's what your advisor/chair did, after all. It's what generations of academics have done. We write for other academics, in a marketplace of ideas that has shelves full to bursting with literature on every imaginable topic. So many academic books and articles are published every year that it is impossible to keep up with them all. Even in fairly "niche" fields (and I won't give examples, for fear of offending, but you can probably come up with a list on your own), it can be difficult to read absolutely everything that's being published.

It's a glorious age of information in which we live, right?

It's also an overwhelming glut of ideas and data.

At the same time, we're in something of an anti-intellectual place in history. I offer this not as a commentary on modern politics (though there are naturally elements of this reflected in politics around the world) and more as a commentary on how very badly those of us in academia tend to communicate what we know to people outside academia. If we only write for other academics, why *wouldn't* people outside academia view us as, for lack of a better word, elitists? Were you ever left out of a clique, not privy to in-jokes, or talked down to? How did that make *you* feel?

This is where the second assumption comes in. If you're doing work that matters, it needs to matter to more than just other scholars. It needs to matter to people who don't have access to university library databases. It needs to offer some sort of insight that improves the life of a human being who neither knows nor cares about the name of the field in which you are receiving your degree, someone for whom "anthropology" and "zoology" are nerd-words that hold no interest, but "stories about people" and "facts about animals" are maybe not just interests, but passions.

The knowledge you produce with your thesis matters. The work you are doing matters, or you wouldn't be doing it.

Think about how you can communicate what you're doing to someone without an advanced degree—someone smart, capable, and motivated to learn interesting things, but without the time, resources, or interest to stay in school as long as you have. Strip out the jargon and find the essence of the story you're telling. Remember that academic writing doesn't need to sound like the things you are forced to read; it's allowed to (and SHOULD!) sound like the things you **want to read**. It ought to sound like something people who know nothing about the field will still find interesting.

Think about how you can share it. Maybe short press paragraphs you can send out to online publications, or digest versions of your thesis you can submit to those publications. Maybe something you could do a podcast episode or a reel or make a meme about. Maybe a series of LinkedIn posts that take what you've done and translate it into something actionable.

Humanize what you're doing. Broaden your audience. Make your work accessible to people who aren't academics. Do your part to make people interested in, maybe even passionate about, learning something new.

Your audience is whomever you want your audience to be.

So make your audience the world.

P.S.: This may be the advice that is most likely to get you into trouble with your chair. The idea that unique and authentic voices need to be heard, and should be heard, can be threatening to some academics (particularly Those of a Particular Age), especially if their identities are twisted into intellectual Gordian knots that make it impossible for them to disentangle themselves from the way *their* mentors told them academic writing ought to sound. To a non-trivial extent, the co-dependent relationship they have with stilted, overblown, polysyllabic rhetoric is Not Your Problem.

Other than in the sense that it is, because you still have to work with them, and they still have some measure of control over the short-term progression of your career. As in almost all such situations, "conversation" will be preferable to "fight," and you should be ready to work to refine your authorial voice at least a little. Helping you do that is part of the chair's job, you know.

Just don't let your chair be your only audience. If you

write a document for them, they will be the only one likely to read it.

~

Summary: Key Points on Writing

You are telling a story. This means you have to hook your reader, and change how they think about something important.

No story of any scope gets written in a single sitting. Don't expect too much of yourself; break the work up into chunks. Once you have all the chunks written, go back and pay more attention to the transitions to make the document flow.

You are not in this by yourself. Make good use of your thesis chair.

You will not get it right the first time, and that's okay. The bulk of writing is re-writing, after all. You will revise until you are sick of revising. Then you will revise some more. You will get angry and frustrated and figure out how to overcome the fact that sometimes, you've written something that isn't very good. Anger at yourself over a bad draft is self-defeating. Use bad drafts to get better.

Edit, and edit, and edit some more. Pay attention to the details. Word choice matters. Sentence clarity matters. Paragraph structure matters. Look at all those levels, and more, when you're editing your work. When you edit, you can actually SEE the document getting better—which is cool. It's a reminder that you are in control of your writing.

If you get blocked, write something else. Writer's block is often your brain having too many things to say at once, or a function of you trying to focus on the wrong thing. If your brain is too busy, consider trying meditation. For me, writing *is* meditation.

Don't try to sound like anybody else, and don't be boring. Be you. It's the only thing that will work, in the end.

PART THE THIRD: PROJECT MANAGEMENT, REDUX

Early on, I pointed out that even if you never write another academic paper, the thesis has value because it gives you project management experience. When you are done, you will have planned and executed a large-scale project. You will have identified, obtained, and coordinated resources. Those resources will include personnel (your chair, your committee, any readers you might have enlisted, and the wonderful administrative staff of your program), the various books and articles you will have cited, the other tools needed to make it through the process (including, but not limited to, software, funding, and the always-important adult beverages), and your personal support network. You will have developed or adopted a timeline, set goals, managed progress, and done all the things that just about any individual who has to take on large-scale tasks as part of their job will have to do. And really, given that you're going to grad school for some form of specialized education, there are probably all sorts of fun and exciting large-scale tasks in your future.

There are a couple of aspects of project management

that I want to focus on as we move toward the end of this book. One is fairly obvious: You've got a lot of administrivia to deal with. If you don't know that word—"administrivia" —it's an inescapable part of life, and reflects all those stupid little tasks that we have to deal with on an administrative level, in order to actually get work done. Administrative trivia. So long as we work for someone else, there will be micro-tasks that really don't seem like they ought to be part of our job. But if we don't do them, nobody else will. And if you work for yourself, you'll probably have even more administrivia. The difference then is that no one will nag you about all the nit-picky stuff that you have to pay attention to.

The administrivia of writing your thesis is largely not that nit-picky. The administrative things you have to do, to finish your thesis and receive your degree, include very important meetings and deadlines and so forth that you need to be aware of. I won't pretend to know what all those things are like in your program, but I will tell you the kinds of things that you need to be paying attention to, if you're going to navigate the process successfully.

So that's one part of project management. Literally managing the project that is your thesis.

The second part is, to me, simultaneously the most important and the most likely to get overlooked. When you're managing the project that is your thesis, you need to continue managing the project that is your life. You have to take care of you.

It's hard. Grad school, as I've said, is a stressful time. It's easy to get so caught up in the work you're doing that you neglect yourself.

If you neglect yourself, though, you won't be at your best. A sluggish body leads to a sluggish mind. Sitting at a computer all day and reading articles and banging away at your thesis may seem like the only way to finish your degree and start the rest of your life.

It is and it isn't. You have to find time to take care of yourself. You have to think about your well-being. You have to get up and go for a walk, or go to the store and buy some fresh fruits and vegetables, or do fifteen minutes of stretching, or even just walk to the window and stand and let yourself ponder the Zen of parking lots for a few minutes. You will still finish, even if you do all of those things, and you will finish as a healthier version of yourself than if you just sat and banged that keyboard for two years.

Having said all that? The "Managing your life" material reflects the advice I either wish I'd been given, or wish I'd paid attention to. I started grad school when I was not quite 22, and as such, I was pretty sure I knew exactly what I did and didn't need to do in order to be successful in school. I'd been successful in school my whole life, and nobody ever had to tell me how! (I seriously believed that, too. I was, in hindsight, an obnoxious know-it-all who was virtually incapable of giving anybody else credit for my success. Don't be like me. I think I was a nice guy, but I was smug without good reason. I do, by the way, recognize the irony of a person who claims to have previously been an obnoxious know-it-all writing a book telling anybody how to do anything. Fortunately, I'm immune to irony's harmful effects. Not in a smug way, though.)

So, you know, it's possible somebody told me all of the things I'm going to tell you about managing the project that is "living your life" while in grad school and that I chose not to hear them. I wish I hadn't gone, "Hey, I'm 22 and have the metabolism of a freaking mountain goat—I don't have to watch what I eat!" Or, "Exercise? I walk from the parking deck to my office and back every day. I'm exercising my brain the rest of the time, and that's what I'm here for!" Or, "Social life? I never had one of those before, so why start now?"

Don't be like me. Take care of yourself during grad school. You will find that the work is easier when you're healthy than when you're not.

That's for later, though. For now, let's talk about the mechanics of managing the thesis project.

Mechanic One: Remember the F(riendly) Manual?

I told you to read it, but we both know that you didn't. Manuals are boring. You may have downloaded it and saved it to your computer, or it may be buried somewhere in your office. Assuming your program has one, open it and look at the table of contents. You'll see topics like "The Thesis Committee" and "The Thesis Meeting" and "Thesis Formatting Requirements," all of which are important and dull and really, you've read this book, so why bother?

You should bother because although I give you advice about various mechanics, I do not know (unless you're one of my students) how those mechanics get implemented at your institution. You need to be aware of the local guidelines, because you—not your chair, not your parents, not your dog—are responsible for following them.

I stand by my earlier recommendation. If you have a manual, keep it handy as you read this book, and do some cross-checking as you go. I can give you general advice, but anything program-specific overrides my guidance.

❧

Mechanic Two: Deadlines

Be aware of the departmental and university deadlines (most will be in the manual...) and meet them, but do not make them your primary targets. Those deadlines are often set as late as it is possible to set them, and still allow students to complete their degree requirements. If you do everything at the last possible minute, you run the risk of not completing on-time and having to pay for another semester's registration.

"Well then, I guess the department ought to move its deadlines sooner!"

Serious question: Why do you feel, at this stage in your life, that you need to depend on someone else to set deadlines for you? Do you think you're going to go through life with somebody else setting deadlines that are as late as they are willing to accept the work from you, and that you'll be fine if you make a habit of getting everything to your boss at the eleventh hour?

It's a strategy you can try, but it's kind of a slow road to mediocrity. People who get ahead, who get promoted, who get recognized, don't wait for someone else to give them deadlines. They find out what they have to do, then they set their own deadlines, bust their asses, and turn in excellent work.

If you were the type of person who wanted to skate by and barely graduate, I don't think you would be in graduate school, much less reading a "how to" book about thesis-writing.

Set your own deadlines. Look at what you have to accomplish, figure out how long you think each element ought to take, discuss it with your chair, and start going after those goals. Don't count on anybody else (including your chair) to set deadlines for you. That's not their job, because this is not their thesis.

~

Mechanic Three: The Meetings

The mechanics of proposing and defending a thesis vary from school to school. I can describe the meetings in general terms, but you really need to find out the local norms and requirements. Depending on your program, you may not have to formally propose your project to a committee. If that's true, skip to the section on "Defending your thesis."

Before I get into the meeting mechanics, though, let me say this: the most important element of the meeting is you. You are the reason everyone is getting together. You have done the work. You know your stuff. Walk into that meeting with CONFIDENCE. Be humble, and don't fool yourself into thinking you know everything—but you have put in the hours. You have done the work. Show confidence.

Even when you don't necessarily feel it.

Proposing your thesis. In some programs—mainly those where the thesis involves collection and analysis of data—two meetings get scheduled with your committee. The first is the proposal, and the second is the defense. The proposal's purpose is to present your planned project to your committee, explain/justify/defend your decisions, and obtain feedback on how you plan to conduct your project.

Depending on your program, the proposal meeting may involve a formal presentation of your research, or it may simply involve an extended question-and-answer session. The presentation is useful in the same sense that every presentation is useful. The more practice you have in presenting ideas to an audience of your peers (many of whom know what you're talking about as well as or better than you do, in the real world), the better your chances of success.

It's also stressful in the same way that every presentation is stressful. If you don't like talking to groups, you'll probably dread this as well. Even though it's a small audience. Even though you more or less hand-picked the audience. Even though you have done months of research to get ready. Typical public speaking phobias apply. Just bear in mind that your committee is not out to get you. They want you to succeed.

Things you need to do in other presentations also apply in the proposal meeting:

Make eye contact.

Pause.

Pay attention to your pacing. If you have a tendency to rush, have a water bottle handy and let yourself sip from it every so often to help slow you down.

And perhaps most importantly, **do not panic**. You invited these folks to take part. They want you to write the best thesis you can. They do not want to watch you crash and burn.

Unless they're jerks. Try not to invite jerks to be on your committee.

The question-and-answer portion of the thesis proposal may start while you're presenting. Unless there are rules for proposals in your program that say, "No questions will be asked until the presentation is complete," expect interruptions.

If there are rules for proposals in your program that say,

"No questions will be asked until the presentation is complete," still expect interruptions.

When you're talking about your literature review, expect to be asked for specifics on what some of the authors you cite said or did, especially if you cited the same sources multiple times. Anticipate that the connections you draw between different authors' work may be unpacked a little, and that you may be asked to justify those connections in more detail. Remember that, when you get a question along those lines, the committee member is almost never trying to trap you. Committee members assume when they ask questions that either you have an answer, can come up with an answer, or are interested in what they think the answer is. As such, consider a response like, "Well, when I think about that connection, my logic is [you know, whatever; some stuff]. Does that clarify my intent?"

One thing you should NOT do is start an answer with, "Well, I'm not sure if this is what you're looking for, but..." Even if the committee member has a certain response in mind, most want to hear what you have to say—not what you think they want you to say. If they disagree with you, this can open up a dialogue. If they disagree in a way that puts them at odds with what your chair believes to be the case, then your chair may step in to provide their perspective after you answer. But you need to answer first.

If you've got hypotheses, expect to be asked to clarify and justify them. A useful activity, in preparing for a proposal meeting, is to look at each hypothesis and ask yourself, "Why might the opposite be true?" That is, come up with a justification for why your hypothesis might be completely wrong, and the exact reverse might be correct. Then figure out how to punch holes in that alternate hypothesis.

If you go in assuming that what you are hypothesiz-ing/arguing is the only way things can be, is the absolute truth, is Definitely So, you are setting yourself up to be knocked down. If you can anticipate the major critiques (and committee members WILL look at your hypotheses and consider the opposite, believe me!) and come up with answers to those critiques, you are setting yourself up to succeed.

The same general advice applies to your methodology. Expect to justify why you want to do the thesis the way you want to do it. If you're in the social sciences, this includes all elements of your study's methodology, including the opera-tionalization of your variables, how you're gathering data—everything. Be familiar with common alternatives to the decisions you made.

At some point, your committee will run out of questions. What usually happens then is that they ask you to step out of the room while they confer privately. When I was a student, it felt kind of like the thing my world history teacher in high school taught us about Egyptian religion, where the soul of the deceased was taken by Anubis and put on a scale against a feather; if the soul weighed more than the feather, the deceased spent eternity in a Very Bad Place. If the soul were lighter than the feather, the deceased instead went to a Very Good Place.

That's all grossly over-simplified and Westernized, and I make no claims to Egyptological accuracy. That's just how it felt, when I was sent out of the thesis meeting to wait.

Reality in that room, it turns out, is much more like the scene in *Bull Durham* where the baseball players gather on the pitcher's mound to conference. Everybody assumes such discussions are very serious and game-related. Thing is, they often aren't.

What happens while you're out of the room? First, discussion of your thesis proposal. Things that need to get changed or clarified. Whether you pass. Then lunch plans. Complaining about course loads. Checking in on how family members are doing. Griping about the weather. Lots of stuff.

We don't do this because we want to torment students. I promise. For the most part, faculty don't get much time to sit and talk and catch up, so sometimes that happens while you're out in the hall, checking your phone and worrying about how we will judge your soul. On behalf of faculty everywhere:

Sorry about that.

Eventually, you'll get called back in and told whether or not you pass. Failing is relatively rare (again, talk to other students in your program for a sense of "how rare" that is), but can happen. Most of the time, there are a bunch of revisions you need to make, sometimes additions to your methodology, sometimes deletions. Having revisions is normal, and if you have things you need to revise, that's not even remotely "failing." I can't recall ever being in a thesis or dissertation meeting that didn't result in a list of changes and revisions. That's just the nature of the process.

Everything your committee requires is designed to improve the quality of your thesis. It's not done to create more work for you, and any work it creates should make this a better project.

Defending your thesis. If you had to propose your thesis before you started, a lot of the pressure should be off. To take the program I taught in as an example, if you (a) did what you said you were going to do, as was agreed to in your proposal meeting by your committee and (b) did not violate any relevant ethics code in conducting your study, you would pass the defense. That's not to say no one got hard questions or that there weren't revisions needed. There are always hard questions, and there are ALWAYS revisions.

It's also not to say that your committee members won't be critical of some of the decisions you made that went beyond what was agreed upon (or decisions to NOT go beyond what was agreed upon), because they will. But I find proposals much more stressful than defenses, because in the proposal you never know what's going to come up as possible changes, nor do you know how much work those changes will require.

Many defenses follow a similar framework to the proposal meeting previously described. The student gives a short presentation on their thesis. If you had a proposal, you can probably skip most of the literature review. Your committee will have now read it twice and heard you talk about it once. That's usually enough. Skip to what's new; remind them of your hypotheses, then review your methodology and focus on your results and the interpretation of those results. (Yes, I've defaulted to a data-centric science-based framework. In other types of programs, different norms obviously apply.)

Expect questions. Other than random nit-pick questions, most of what you ought to expect has to do with interpretation. You're done, so what does it all mean? What can you conclude? What contribution does your work make?

Now, if you're in a program where you don't have to formally propose, and the defense is the first time you sit down with your committee, things are potentially a little different.

And when I say "different" I mean "more stressful, by a lot." You've done all the work, drawn all your conclusions, and now you're going to be presenting the finished product to the committee you selected. People who may have had no say in the process and no solid idea of why you did what you did now have a chance to pick your work apart.

Sound terrifying? Welcome to academia, where you work hard on something, then people sit in judgment on the quality of your work without an appreciation of your process.

Wait, that's not just academia. That's "life."

My bad.

Anyway, the core of any proposal or defense (also, "life") is preparation. Go back over your key sources. Try to find the holes in your arguments, and how to fill them. If you've got a presentation, practice it. Have people ask you questions that make no sense. Talk to your dog. (Not your cat. Your cat won't care. Your dog will listen to you and look confused, and that's good preparation for the face committee members make when they're trying to come up with the right way to ask you a question.)

There is fear that goes along with putting an idea "out there." You care about your thesis or you wouldn't be writing it. The topic matters to you. You will, inevitably, have some ego-involvement, and you will get critiqued, and your ego will get bruised.

In life, you either come up with ideas that risk being shot down, or you exist in a state of boring mediocrity. Not every idea you have will be great. Not every section of your thesis will be great, or even good. But you get better by getting critiqued and learning how to address critiques. As long as you don't take it personally (and generally, you shouldn't), you'll be fine.

The fear prior to and during a proposal/defense is normal. It's okay.

Be your own worst critic. Preparing for your thesis

proposal or defense is partly a function of knowing what the meeting is going to be like, mechanically, and partly a function of getting yourself in the right head-space. You're going to be asked questions. People whose classes you've taken, people that you want to think well of you, will ask questions that feel like threats to your professional identity and/or your sanity.

That's the bad news. The good news is, you can prepare. And to me, the most helpful preparation involved (1) re-reading my thesis, from front to back, and (2) asking this question:

"If I wanted to rip my own thesis apart, how would I go after it?"

Part of your job, as a critical thinker and a builder of arguments, is to anticipate criticism. You have chosen how to write your document. Others will disagree with your decisions, with your definitions, and with your attempt to approach the question as you have at all.

Your thesis committee won't be out to break your will and destroy your life, but you still need to think about what kinds of questions they may ask. Hearing a question that you anticipated actually get asked in the meeting does a couple of things, right off the bat.

First, it reminds you that you really do know your stuff, and that you were ready for this. Will you anticipate all the questions? No. But this one? You GOT this one.

Second, being able to say, "You know, I was thinking about this last night, and here's what I came up with..." makes you LOOK really smart and prepared.

Know your stuff inside-out. I said it before, and it's worth repeating: Go in confident, but humble. Talk with your chair ahead of time about what to expect. Talk with your fellow grad students ahead of time about what to expect. And remember that it's just, in most cases, two hours out of your life. You will live through it. You will be fine.

Enough about mechanics. What about that "life" thing?

∼

Managing Your Life, Part 1: Don't Get Mad at Yourself

Some days, the words won't come easily. You'll get frustrated. You'll hate life, but not as much as you hate grad school. You'll probably do some crying.

This is normal. Even if you follow every bit of advice I give (which you shouldn't—not every bit of advice applies to everyone), you will find that times when you just can't believe how little you've accomplished.

Don't take it out on yourself. You are doing your best. Some days, your mind gets stuck. When the writing isn't happening, do the other things that have to get done. Format the document. Organize references. Search for more sources. Re-read a key article. Do something productive, because even if you write no new text today, you will get the chance to write new text again tomorrow.

Anger at yourself doesn't solve anything. Just in general, anger doesn't solve much. You can get mad at me, for writing a book that I warned you was going to be full of well-intentioned crap, especially if I give advice that doesn't end up fitting your program or your project.

You can get mad at your chair. Most of us know that at some point, we will piss you off. We will tell you to do something in one draft, then change our minds and tell you to do the exact opposite in the next. Or you'll slave over a revision, send it to us, and we'll send it back with minimal notes other than, "Awkward—re-word for clarity" out in the margins.

Getting mad at anybody, yourself included, is normal. But it also distracts you. It works you up and pulls your focus away from the thesis.

Don't stay mad at yourself, when the writing isn't going well. Recognize that you're angry, recognize that it's probably about frustration, and let it go.

You will get your thesis written, and when you do, the frustrating days will fade. Oh, and...

Quit comparing yourself to other students' progress and other chairs' processes. You need to focus on doing you. If you somehow made a mistake in selecting your chair, and have the option of changing, this ought to be a conversation the two of you have. But if you hear a member of your cohort talking about how they got glowing feedback and are so happy to be working with Dr. Whomever, that doesn't mean that you would be getting glowing feedback if you changed chairs, nor does it mean that they would be getting terrible feedback if they were working with your chair.

It really and truly doesn't matter what anybody else is doing. It only matters what you are doing. Focus on you, and on your thesis. Graduate school is, when done right, not a competition.

Impostor syndrome and you. "Impostor syndrome" is the sense that we aren't as good as people believe we are, and that eventually, they're going to figure us out. In this context, it's the little voice in your head that says, "You can only fake this grad school thing for so long before they figure out that you don't really belong here."

Spoiler: that voice is a damned liar.

There's a lot of research on impostor syndrome. I am going to cite exactly none of it. To me, although research is always important, at its core impostor syndrome is just a human problem that smart people are particularly likely to experience. Now, my one nod to the research literature has to be to acknowledge that, due to cultural messaging, there are absolutely some groups whose members are more likely to experience impostor syndrome. I'm going to restrict my discussion to the context of grad school and grad students, though—and that makes a focus on this as something thoughtful people are more likely to experience appropriate.

Let me start with a story. I mentioned earlier that I was a smug little jerk when I started grad school, convinced that I knew how to be successful. Getting to grad school and being around SO MANY really smart people, though?

It started to make me feel like maybe all I was really good at was taking standardized tests. I rocked the GRE and looked great on paper, but what if taking tests was all I could do? I looked around and saw other students publishing more articles than I was, presenting at more conferences than I did, networking more effectively than I could, and I thought, "I'm not as good as they think I am—and soon, they're going to figure that out."

I was terrified. Then I was at a meeting where one of the other grad students—a student who I think may have already been on the job market, may have already had a job, and definitely had a solo-author publication in one of the top journals in our field—talked about how she felt like she wasn't as good as everybody thought she was, and that they were eventually going to figure it out.

And everybody in the room nodded.

It wasn't just me. It was also this super-successful, talented, amazing student that I could only aspire to be— and almost everyone else.

Here's the thing: as an intelligent, thoughtful person, you are able to imagine your own potential. You are able to see things that you didn't do as well as you might have liked, places where you could have performed better, and when you think about those things, you trick yourself into believing that you aren't performing up to your potential.

What you are forgetting is that NO ONE ELSE CAN SEE INSIDE YOUR HEAD. No one else knows what you *didn't* do, that you *maybe could have* done. They know what you did, and they are likely impressed with what they saw. And if they aren't, and tell you, "You can do better," that's the clearest possible indication that they already know what I'm about to say.

You are not an impostor. You are in graduate school because you worked hard, and because intelligent people reviewed your application and said, "Yes, [$studentname] would be a good member of our program." And they admitted you. You *belong* where you are. You *earned* it.

Got it? Good. Now tell your impostor syndrome to go to hell. Mine will be waiting at the gates to greet it.

Managing Your Life, Part 2: Stressed Yet?

I joke about a lot of things. It's a defense mechanism. You put something in front of me that's uncomfortable and I will make fun of it. I'm sure my clinical colleagues would have various explanations for this behavior. I'm engaging in this bit of unsolicited self-disclosure because I also joke around about the stress of grad school and writing your thesis. If my joking around bothers you, then you really need to read this section. If my joking around makes you chuckle, I'm good with that. It's kind of my preference.

To say that grad school is stressful (as I have...) is a pretty colossal understatement, right? You completed twelve-ish years of primary school. You've got an undergraduate degree that took somewhere between three and five years to finish. You've been in school pretty much your entire life, but all of that? That was the warm-up. That was you learning all the stuff that you needed to learn in order to get ready to learn the stuff that's going to define who you are for the rest of your life.

Morrie? Not helping.

Of course I'm not helping! I'm saying what that obnoxious little jerk of a voice in the back of your mind says, when you're lying in bed and can't sleep because you have no idea how to prioritize everything you have to do, how to find the hours in the day to read what you have to read and write what you have to write, how you can even stop to think about whether you're eating right (you probably aren't) or exercising enough (see prior parenthetical), and if you are managing to eat right and exercise enough, you're probably feeling guilty about it because that's taking time that you aren't putting into the things that you're being graded on and OH MY SWEET GOD(DESS) HOW AM I EVER GOING TO GET THROUGH THIS HELL THAT I CHOSE FOR MYSELF??!?!!

Which is to say, almost everybody who goes through graduate school goes through exactly what you are experiencing. That person who looks like she has her crap together? She doesn't. That other one, who looks like he never has to work hard and always has something insightful to say in class? He hasn't slept in three days.

Everybody around you is JUST AS MESSED UP AS YOU ARE.

And that's okay. You are all going through this together. Not only are you sharing this experience with others, you are doing it under the tutelage of people who have been through the exact same progression, and came out the other side, and generally have no desire to make you miserable. (Standard caveats apply here: Some people are lunatic sadist ass-hats. Some of those LSAs do, in fact, go into academia. However, it is unlikely that every faculty member in your department is an LSA. Most of us care very much about your well-being. I promise.)

The stress level is higher now because you're asked to do things—like, you know, write a thesis—that you have probably never done before. The classes aren't like undergraduate classes. The assignments are longer and more challenging. Ergo, stress.

What do you do about it?

Talk to people. And by "people" I mean, you know—human beings. Texting with friends and family is fine, emailing is okay—but that's not human contact. One of the things graduate school often does to folks is make them feel isolated.

Don't let it. Keep the connections. If you have a grad student who is your mentor/big sibling/whatever term gets used where you are, use that person. They've already been through some variation of what you're going through. They can help. You're probably part of a cohort who are going through the same things you're going through. Talk to them. Commiserate.

Everyone who goes to grad school needs a support network. Build one. Other students are the best place to start. They fundamentally get it. But when you let yourself go other places where people with similar interests gather—places like concerts, gaming stores, group fitness classes, book clubs, dog parks, and so forth—you can further expand your support network, and even remind yourself that, yes, there really is life outside (and after!) grad school. That's a benefit of talking to people.

"People" still includes your chair, by the way. Talk to them as well. The meetings where a student comes in and goes through half the box of Kleenex we keep on our desk aren't our favorites, because we want you to be happy and successful. But if you need to cry, cry! Talk through what's going on (school-related or not—we can't help with things we don't know about, but can't and won't force you to disclose anything you're not comfortable sharing) and see what we have to say. Sometimes, just the act of talking through the problems helps. Or, at least, that's what psychotherapists say.

In our department, the administrative assistants pride themselves on being surrogate mothers for our grad students. A clear message during orientation is, "You can come talk to us—and we always have chocolate."

If none of the people around your department feel safe to you, for whatever reason, then look at other resources on campus. You ought to have access to some form of wellness/counseling center. Call them and make an appointment. Tell them you're a grad student. This is important, because (a) they are very aware of how stressful grad school is, and (b) if you happen to be a grad student in psychology or counseling, they can make sure that if there are other students from your department/program who work in the center, you won't get scheduled with them.

The folks whose job it is to help you will do everything in their power to help you.

So find out what your resources are and make an appointment. There's nothing wrong with that.

You are not alone. I've known people who came out of grad school severely clinically depressed, in part because of all the stress.

Well, let me qualify that. When I say "I've known" people who suffered from depression in grad school, what I really mean is, "That was me."

I don't blame graduate school for my depression. My neurotransmitters were out of whack. I don't know what made my serotonin levels get screwy, but I know it happened towards the end of my time in grad school, just like it did towards the end of my time in high school. Faced with a job I had to start before I finished my dissertation, the prospect of leaving some of the best friends I'd made since elementary school, and the need to move hundreds of miles, I was stressed. And then there was a disruption to my data collection that delayed me starting my new job for an entire semester and had me writing the last chapters of my dissertation during my first semester as a new faculty member. Everything piled up, my neurotransmitters rebelled, and life became overwhelming.

When you're depressed, it's hard to remember what life was like for your non-depressed brain. That makes it hard to imagine that the depression is ever going to end. Graduate school, with deadlines and stressors and shiny new challenges, is a breeding ground for the kinds of thoughts that skip merrily alongside depression and anxiety.

If you are worried about yourself, ask for help. Talk to your friends and colleagues. Make that appointment with the counseling center. Graduate school makes you feel alone, but you aren't. If you believe you are, that's the part of your brain that has stopped being able to see the end goal, and is trying to isolate you from people who can help you finish.

Ask for help, and believe in yourself. Have faith in yourself. If you're religious, talk to someone at your place of worship. If you're not, talk to someone you like and respect.

You can do this. People believe in you. You were NOT a mistake in the grad school admissions process, so tell your impostor syndrome to STFU. You deserve to be here, because you are bright and talented. Life is a series of accomplishments that we never imagined we could achieve. You lost that perspective through your sixteen-ish years of schooling prior to grad school, because all of the accomplishments for those years built incrementally. You took a class, you took another class, you took tests, you figured out how to "game" multiple choice questions, you wrote essays that met the requirements of the assignment, and you fell into a comfortable routine. Then grad school took that routine, froze it with liquid nitrogen, and hit it with a big freaking hammer.

You can do this. Trust someone who's been there and came out the other side.

Managing Your Life, Part 3: Self-Care

Grad school is a microcosm of life. I've said as much a few times because it's important; you are transitioning from "pure student" mode to "professional" mode by taking a step not a lot of folks take as a "student-professional." People expect a lot out of you in both grad school and life, and there's no simple instruction manual for either. Even this book, for all that I hope it's helpful, doesn't qualify as an "instruction manual." It's more or less what I wanted it to be: advice and observations about one of the most stressful and rewarding elements of the graduate school process—the thesis—which I hope will also give you tools to be successful in your career.

Some things that are easy to forget, as you deal with the stressors that get introduced to (or heightened in) your life during grad school, are related to caring for yourself.

Eat well. Up to this point in your life, you may have been able to get away with shoveling whatever horrific fast food was handy into your face. You may have developed a fondness for alcohol. I'm not going to tell you that you have to cut out fast food (you should, though) or that you ought to stop drinking (especially when I only learned about Sapphire and tonics in grad school...). I will say two things instead. First, eating healthy has immediate benefits, in terms of energy level, focus, and general brain-power, that will help you in a variety of ways. Second, in not too many years, your metabolism will stop being able to keep up with those eating and drinking habits, and the calories you put into your body won't magically disappear.

Fresh food makes you feel better, when you eat it, than carb-laden calorie bombs. Don't get me wrong—I love donuts. Love love LOVE. And paczki season? Oh my. (If you're not from Michigan or Ohio, just Google "paczki." Then be happy you can't get them where you live. Or sad, depending.) But those carb bombs give you short bursts of energy, followed by a crash. Going for something more balanced—protein, fruits, vegetables, nuts—offers a lot of health benefits and, again, makes you feel good. It's more work to prep fresh food, and definitely more expensive to go out and have someone else prepare super-organic, responsi-bly-raised, cruelty-free meals, but the thing about the extra work that goes with prepping better food is that it forces you to take a break and be right there, in the moment, taking care of yourself. The more you take care of yourself, the better you will feel.

Writing a thesis takes months. Cooking a meal? If you get extravagant, maybe a couple of hours. Putting together a salad takes about as much time as it requires to open a bag of greens, chop up some carrots/tomatoes/whatever, toss in some deli ham or turkey, sprinkle on some cheese, and pour the dressing. Before grad school, I never touched salads. During grad school, I met my culinary brother, who claimed an allergy to chlorophyll. Despite his influence, by the end of grad school I'd come to appreciate, even love, a good salad.

I suppose that, rather than saying "eat well," I could just say, "Don't eat crap." Personally, I'm amazed how much better I've felt since I lowered my crap intake and raised my vegetable intake.

It's not just me, either. Research has consistently shown that lifestyle choices, including diet, can affect not just our physical health but also our mental health, with poor eating and its physical consequences potentially contributing to the kinds of depression and anxiety students often experience (see Krusselbrink Flatt, 2013)—and as we all know, mental health challenges for students have only increased in recent years. For other reading on the effects of diet on students, studies like Pollitt and Mathews (1998) and Taras (2005) are included in my references, if you want to look them up. With student wellness programs becoming more common, focusing on healthy eating (even if it's not always the most popular topic; see Futch, Gordon, & Gerdes, 2025) is key.

Exercise. This is a "do as I say, not as I did" section, because in grad school I did lamentably little exercising. There were gyms on campus that I could have used, and some of my friends were regulars. I went to the gym a few times, but never felt like I knew what I ought to be doing. Ride a bike some? Uh, sure. Lift something? Okay. I can do that. I had free weights in my room in high school. Didn't know how to use them properly, but had them.

I didn't exercise as much as I should have in high school, or college, or grad school, nor did I really exercise as much as I ought to until I got to my mid-thirties. And damn, I wish I'd exercised more when I was younger! I went from being the kid who played all the sports when he was little, to the kid who played baseball until he was fifteen, to the kid who decided that he needed to focus on grades rather than sports. After I quit baseball, I spent my summers on the couch reading, eating pretzels or cheesy poofs, and watching bad movies.

You will feel better if you exercise. I mean, even with the occasional pain or soreness, exercise is good for your body. Staying active, particularly when you've got the "job" of grad student that requires you to sit and read, and the "job" of thesis author that requires you to sit and stare at a computer screen with your hands hovering over a keyboard, will help keep you sane.

Take a couple of yoga classes. Go on a run. Get a balance ball chair and every once in a while, push back from your desk and do some crunches on it. Play intramural sports. Do *anything* other than just sitting, reading, writing, and eating. It takes time, but it also gives you the energy you need to get work done, and again, there's science to support this. For example, Bland, Melton, Bigham, and Welle (2014) found that vigorous physical activity, stretching, and strength training could all help college students cope with stress.

Scully, Kremer, Meade, Graham, and Dudgeon (1998) offer a great review of the effects physical exercise has on various aspects of psychological well-being, including depression, anxiety, stress, and so forth. Again—science!

Eating better and exercising take time, but also increase the quality of the time you spend working. A healthy person can and will predictably get more done and have improved focus and so forth than a less healthy person.

Sleep, dammit! There's this idea that grad students are so busy they never sleep, and that if you're sleeping, you're somehow doing grad school wrong. I'll be delicate here: that's bullshit. You need sleep. Your body needs time to recover. You need to not be "on" all the time.

I'm not telling you when to sleep; maybe you're nocturnal and don't get rolling until after 10, when everybody else in the world stops sending emails. If so, stay up to all hours and sleep in (class schedule permitting). If you're a morning person, get to bed early and get up earlier. But get at least 6-8 hours of sleep a night whenever possible.

Practice good time management so that you can get enough sleep. You've got a lot of responsibilities, but for cryin' out loud, the most important responsibility is to yourself. You can wear yourself down to nothing during grad school, give yourself ulcers, end up depressed and anxious —even if you sleep enough. Sleeping less just compounds all of the things going on in your life and makes it harder to deal with them because you're fatigued.

And yes, I will toss a little science at you again. We'll just go with Trockel, Barnes, and Egget (2000), who showed a linkage between sleep and GPA. Now, GPA isn't the be-all of grad school, but if you can't get the grades, you won't stick around long enough to finish the thesis.

Take care of yourself. Don't fall into the trap of, "If I

sleep one hour less every night for a year, that's 365.25 extra hours, which is the same as over 15 extra days of productivity each year!" Because that assumes that (a) your productivity in that extra hour will be equivalent to the productivity you have in an hour on full sleep (it won't) and (b) that your productivity in the other hours will not suffer as a result of the increased fatigue that comes with sleeping an hour less (it will).

Have a hobby to take your mind off school. One of the things I regret about my time in grad school is that I stopped writing fiction. Coming out of undergrad, I had a literary agent representing a science fiction book I'd written. About six months into grad school, the stress overwhelmed me and I emailed my agent to tell her that I just wasn't able to divide my focus enough to continue to write fiction, and that I probably ought to focus just on my studies.

It felt like the right decision at the time. Now I'm less certain.

We all have something that fills us with joy, that helps us relax when life gets hard. For me, it was writing. (Still is.) Maybe for you it's dancing, or hiking. Rock climbing. Biking. Collecting sports cards. Writing a pop culture blog. Making silly videos. Gaming. Whatever it is, hold onto it during grad school. If you stop doing something you love, then whatever you do in its place can make you angry, bitter, or sad. You don't want grad school to do that. You are studying things that you want to be studying! Things that excite you! If you use those things to supplant other things that you've loved since childhood (and don't give me any of that "put away your childish things" garbage—if we let go of the things we love from childhood, we lose an important part of ourselves), you will start to hate your chosen field and career.

Let yourself have a hobby. Make time for it. A big part of graduate school, and writing your thesis, is time management. But "time management" isn't "scheduling something to work on every waking hour." It's "scheduling when I'm going to work and when I'm going to relax." There's a reason we talk about work-life balance, after all. You still get to have a life—even during grad school.

Take a day off. This one may get some disagreement, and that's okay. It worked for me—though there's a caveat.

When I started college, my orientation week involved a group of us being assigned to a senior who would give us advice about how to navigate/survive/succeed. I don't remember his actual name, because he went by "Bud," and really, he kind of looked and acted like a "Bud." Bud told us about college, about things to beware of, about things to try. He was one of the upper-level students who accompanied our group on our bonding excursion (we went spelunking, which was amazing!) and who would, for some members of our group, become a supplier of beer. I'll let you guess his brand of choice.

I don't remember much of what Bud told us. Not because of beer (I don't like beer, and never have), but because it's been over thirty years. One thing did stick with me, though.

"Take a day off," he said. "You'll have a lot of work to do, and a lot of freedom for when to do it. It is possible to work every day. The professors give you that much to do. But you'll burn yourself out. I've seen it." He paused at this point to make eye contact with each of us, to make sure we were paying attention. "The best thing you can do, to keep from burning out, is to take a day off every week. Don't work on your papers, don't read for class. Just take a day for you. I like Saturdays myself, but some folks like Sundays. The whole 'sabbath' thing." He shrugged. "One day off makes the other six a lot easier."

Okay, only the first four words are a quote. The rest? My best guess, but 100% the spirit of Bud's message.

I don't know that anybody gave me advice about not-working before Bud, and it's not advice I ever heard during grad school. I'd kind of assumed, in fact, that working all the time was what I was supposed to do. In high school, I didn't date. I studied. When I had a test, I spent hours going over and over my notes. When I had to write a paper, I wrote a draft early enough that my dad could read it and I could revise it based on his feedback. If I didn't have anything else due, I'd read a book. It wasn't until my junior year or so that I even started having phone conversations with people I could potentially date, and I only went to prom because a friend asked me.

So when I say that the idea of taking a day off from school was a revelation, I'm not exaggerating. I did it (Saturdays, other than right before finals week, I got nothing constructive done), then kept doing it in grad school. And other than the whole "depression" thing, I made it through grad school feeling pretty good.

Now, the caveat. Technically, it took me 5.5 years to finish. I had to stay an extra semester to finish my data collection. I don't think that taking a day off each week caused that semester delay; what caused it most directly was a change in the department's policies for recruiting student participants.

So... if you hadn't taken that day off each week, could you have started your data collection even earlier?

That's possible, and I can't say for sure. But looking back, I wouldn't have done anything differently when it comes to days off. There were almost certainly other things I did that extended my completion timeline, but giving myself one weekend day off every week, to go hang out with friends, play cards, watch movies, and whatever else, kept me from feeling quite as isolated as I think I could have.

Self-care and work-life balance don't start being a concern when you're drawing a paycheck. They're relevant as soon as you have sufficient responsibilities that if you don't pay attention to balancing them against your personal life, your personal life can disappear. For most people, that doesn't happen during their undergrad years. Most folks who go to grad school had positive, sometimes even easy, undergraduate experiences. Grad school is where you need to start figuring out who you're going to be, and again, is an advantage of being a student-professional. Learn to take time for yourself, or grad school can eat your life and set you up for workaholism for the next forty years.

The thesis is important, and it will get done. Nothing is as important as your emotional, mental, and physical well-being.

∾

Managing Your Life: The Sweary Bits

To me, profanity IS a form of self-care. This is your warning.

This section relates to (but is not derived from) at least some research on taboo words/swearing/profanity. That literature identifies multiple categories of swearing, including "cathartic swearing." Among other things, cathartic swearing helps relieve tension. This is what I found (and find) swearing to be most helpful for. If you're interested in the research on swearing, Finn (2017) offers a nice overview.

Anyway, the first half-dozen or so drafts of this book were FULL of profanity. Even the title had the word "shit" in it.

I decided, as I started the final round of revisions, that this did not help me craft a book that would reach everyone, or that everyone would find useful/be willing to tolerate. My amusement (and, I'll admit, some amount of bitterness at the inculcated processes/rites of passage that go along with the traditions of grad school) and need to vent my spleen, liver, and part of a kidney, are ultimately less important to me than this book being accessible to everyone. So up to this point, I've been at least relatively well-behaved and kept most of the profanity to myself.

Until now. This section gets all of the swearing. If you don't like profanity, you're probably already bothered by that third paragraph. If you clutched your pearls at the "bullshit" in the prior section, I would advise you to skip this one. If you were raised better than I was (I love my parents, and believe they did a great job raising three kids, but any parenting quality metric that included "never swears around children" is one that would not have led to high marks for them), you may not need the sweary affirmations and advice that follow.

You see, I believe that sometimes, socially-improper vocalizations and the expression of negative emotions through creative use of scatological or other bio-functional language is a healthy way to release tension. I feel that the emotions that go along with the thesis process are sufficiently intense that we need a way to release them. Yes, you can scream into pillows, or punch the heavy bag, or work out at a crossfit box until you dislocate your duodenum and leave grad-student-shaped sweat stains on the rubber floor.

You can also swear. It feels surprisingly good, some-times, and offers no duodenal risk whatsoever.

Here are some of my favorites, then, and why I love them:

Fuck this fucking shit. Has there ever been a better "catch-all" phrase to express grievous dissatisfaction with the state of life/existence? It's so evocative! So succinct! And, as an added bonus, the only non-swear word in the sentence is STILL an anagram of a useful and descriptive bit of profanity.

There will be days when you look at what you're working on—whether it's a draft on your screen, a pile of (real or virtual) articles, an outline, a bunch of tracked changes from your chair—and just want to throw up your hands, run out into the snow, and bury yourself in a pile of frozen whiteness forever. On those days, "Fuck this fucking shit" is a lovely way to express the need to distance yourself from work that has become a little too all-consuming, and to recognize that in the end, you are allowed to walk away from it for a little while. Yes, you'll eventually come back, but for now?

Fuck this fucking shit.

This is unbelievable bullshit. As you move through the writing process, this may become a go-to. Read a dumb arti-cle? Unbelievable bullshit. Library can't procure a key resource, and Google is failing you? Unbelievable bullshit. Wrote a sentence last night and don't know what it means this morning? Unbelievable (and probably delete-able) bull-shit. Advisor tells you to change a paragraph so that it reads almost exactly how it read three drafts ago, un-doing hours of trying to revise to sound like something they would have written and going back to the perfectly-fine and clear enun-ciation of the point you originally drafted? Unbelievable bullshit! (Okay... that one is at least a little bit believable. Still bullshit, but based on my lived experience, believable bullshit. Advisors are human too. Nobody gets everything right on the first pass.)

The world is full of bullshit. It's okay to call it out as such. It's also necessary to bear in mind that, having labeled it, it still has to get dealt with. The labeling feels good, at least.

That bastard wants to ruin my fucking life. You may think I'm talking about your chair. I'm not. The thing about your chair is that they actually have something invested in you. Time, funding, ego—things that matter to them. Can they ruin your life? I mean, yes. Technically. But the motivation to do so is not particularly strong, unless they're the kind of person for whom intellectual self-flagellation has aphrodisiac qualities.

There will be times that it FEELS like your chair wants to ruin your life, when you really ought to be done, when there's no reason to do another draft, when there isn't a reason in the GOD-DAMNED WORLD why the section that you just re-wrote needs to be re-written again, and why the HELL would you need to go and find MORE SOURCES when the ones you have are the most critical sources in the field that EVERY-DAMNED-BODY cites?

In the moment, it feels like a setback. It feels like an attack. It feels like shit.

In almost every case, though, your chair is trying to set you up to be more successful. Not less. If you do well, if you go out and look good, you make them look good. Academics piss themselves over being able to trace their lineage. I mean, thanks to the internet I can trace my academic lineage back to Newton (yes, Isaac) and Leibniz. Which is totally irrelevant to my field, what with me being a psychologist and all.

Anyway, if our academic ancestors matter, our academic offspring matter as well. You matter to your chair.

The people who want to ruin your life are the random assholes you meet along the way who have an axe to grind with a system you just happen to be part of. Some faculty members get a kick out of taking a bunch of grad students— young adults who have consistently been at the top of their classes—and writing tests or other assignments that these super-smart young people will fail. It's a flex for them, a way to show that they really are smarter than all the other people getting advanced degrees. Getting a bad grade in a graduate class won't ruin your life, but when it's done because somebody never dealt with being passed over for Phi Beta Kappa, or never got the exact job that they wanted because there were always slightly-better candidates? That sucks.

And then you may have committee members who just like being dicks in proposal or defense meetings, and who enjoy showing up to job interviews with faculty candidates and asking the most arcane bullshit questions to try to throw the person off, JUST BECAUSE THEY CAN.

Again, it's nerd-flexing. Usually, these types have such abysmally low self-esteem that they just want everybody else to feel like shit as well, and they're big enough assholes to target grad students—probably because the same kind of thing happened to them.

Look, I've said variations on it before, but grad school is hard enough without people piling their decades-old trauma on top of you, and perpetuating stupid systems that in a lot of cases look like academic hazing.

The good news is, a lot of this "old guard" who feel like

they need to gatekeep graduate degrees are retiring. It's just that cultures like the one that enabled this crap take a while to change. They can, though.

If you run into one of these jackasses, recognize them for what they are. Know that they are going to be pedantic puddles of rectal discharge not because they hate you, but because that's who they were trained to be. Work with your chair, and your fellow grad students, to (a) avoid such individuals and (b) commiserate about them over the socially-accepted and legal mind-altering substance of your choice. But don't validate their bullshit.

Or, you know: fuck that fucking shit.

Fuck my life. This is a natural one that I'm pretty sure every grad student says with depressing regularity. If you're the typical/traditional student, you started a 2- or 5-year graduate program when you were in your early 20s. This means that not only did you just commit to more school, when friends you graduated with are out making money, you are looking at anywhere from 10% to 25% of the TOTAL TIME YOU'VE BEEN ALIVE that you have to put up with this shit.

Ergo, "fuck my life" becomes an easy refrain. It will feel, sometimes, as if you have fucked your life.

You haven't. I promise. You made the decision to go on for more education because there is something you wanted to learn, or do, that you could not (a) learn or do on your own, or (b) learn or do without specialized training beyond what your undergrad degree offered. And yes, it feels like a FUCKING LOT, as you start the process, and take your first grad classes, and ponder the writing of a thesis for the first time.

Because it is. No bullshit. It's a lot to do.

But it's something you chose because you care about

what you're going to learn, and what it lets you do. It's a short and intense period of training during which you learn a helluva lot about a specialized area, develop core professional skills and judgment, and find new levels of resilience as you overcome any and all grad-school challenges. Periods where training is intense and information load is high are naturally stressful. They just are.

You will come out the other side, though, and your life should be better for you having done it.

Can I promise it absolutely will? Of course not. But taking two years, or five years, while you're young, to learn a shit-ton of stuff about something you're interested in? Other than the part where you're not making money, tell me how that's worse than spending two years or five years in a job that doesn't end up being what you do for the rest of your life. (Yes, the "not making money" part stinks. That's why I excluded it.)

It's fine to say, "Fuck my life" when things get stressful. Everybody does. Just don't start believing that you've fucked your life. Although that certainly happens to people, it usually doesn't have anything to do with going to grad school.

Fuckity fuck-fuckers that fucking fuck with every-fucking-thing, fucking shithead dickbrained fucknuggets full of bastardized ball-sac sweat, smeared with an unctuous mix of shit and smegma and walking around like goddamned pimples that need to be lanced, boils on the ass of a rancid donkey carcass, ass-faced ditch-licking fish-faced frog-fuckers who wouldn't know what quality looked like if it sat on their fucking faces and sang every verse in the fucking hymnal in pig-fucking-latin!

I don't know about you, but I think this one pretty much speaks for itself. Feel free to use it next time you wrap your little toe around the leg of a coffee table at five in the morning.

I could keep going (don't believe me? I had to consciously stop myself after "frog-fuckers" or that list of obscene hyphenates would still be going), but I think I've more than made my point. Which is not, "Swear early, swear often."

It's that you will get mad, and you will want to swear, and it's okay to do so. But recognize why you're mad. Recognize that the things that are making you mad may not be about you, and that almost all of them are temporary.

Profanity is nice as a release, because just like the things that piss us off are transitory, when we swear the words are present for an instant—and then they're gone. (It ought to go without saying, but I'll say it: avoid live microphones during periods of hyper-expressive vocalization.) If you can cope with those short-term irritations without swearing, good for you. You're a better person than I am!

Summary: Key Points on Project Management

You are managing the "project" that is your thesis, and that means figuring out all the administrivia that goes along with project management. So, congrats on that.

A lot of the administrivia that you have to know about is contained in the student handbook or manual that I told you to read a while ago. You probably didn't. That's okay. Do it now.

You need to take control of your deadlines. Know when your program's deadlines are, then ignore them. Set deadlines well ahead of those deadlines, and meet the ones YOU set. It's a good habit to get into.

Know about the formal, thesis-related meetings. Find out how many there are and what their format will be. Ask questions. Prepare. Recognize that everyone gets nervous about these meetings, and determine that you will kick ass.

Manage your life like it's the most important thing. Because it is. Life doesn't stop happening when you start grad school, or start writing a thesis. You will get frustrated, but don't take it out on yourself. Keep working. Eye on the prize!

You will most likely experience impostor syndrome. Recognize that almost everyone around you also experiences it, and almost NO ONE around you is actually an impostor. You are here for a reason. You can do this.

Everyone gets stressed. You won't be any different. When you need help, ask for it.

Eat well. You will feel better and be more productive than if you live on coffee and fast food. Drink more water. Fruits and vegetables are your friends.

So is exercise. You're going to spend a lot of time sitting and reading and writing, so make sure to take time to get out and DO SOMETHING. Physical activity is worth the time investment.

Sleep. No, for real. You want your mind sharp. Getting enough sleep is critical.

Take some time off. Have a hobby. Give yourself breaks.

Things will make you angry. If it helps, swear. If it really helps, swear a lot. But remember that grad school is a very brief time in your life, and you are also allowed to enjoy it. You are bright, and motivated, and going to be successful. You, my friend, have totally freaking got this.

AFTERWORD: WHY WRITING
MATTERS

I t feels like there have been a lot of news stories, social media posts, and various other forms of commentary about the state of our educational systems, the decline in critical thinking, and how writing is becoming a "lost art."

All of this makes me incredibly sad. (Yes, intentional adverb is intentional!) The idea of writing becoming a lost art makes me saddest, but it's all tied together.

The thing that each of us brings to the table, when it comes to school, work, and life, is the unique way we see the world. Your brain, by virtue of being *your brain*, experiences things in a way that is related to, but distinct from, how every other brain that exists (or ever has existed, or ever will exist) experiences them. You will make connections no one else makes, have thoughts no one else has. You will come up with fresh, exciting ideas. This is what makes humans such wonderful creatures: we gather data from the world around us, and we use it to make sense of that world. We tell ourselves the story of the world, and we fight like hell to find ways for that story to hold together.

It's not an accident that I'm back to the "story" metaphor

here at the end. Telling stories is what we do. It's the core of our human experience. We learn from stories, we believe in stories, and we think of our lives in the same kind of terms we use when we think about stories. From Tolstoy to TikTok, stories are how we understand ourselves and one another.

When we write, we share our stories. The more clear and persuasive the story you tell, the more it integrates different ideas and perspectives in novel ways, the greater impact your writing will have.

And the more you write, the more you practice telling your stories, shaping them and re-shaping them, finessing them and cutting them and screaming at them to JUST BE A LITTLE MORE PERFECT, the more clearly you see the world. The more words you put on paper/the screen, the more you find or create order in what you see around you. The more you practice silent communication, the easier it becomes to sit down and have a conversation in which you can critically evaluate a situation and poke at it until you find a way to solve an apparently un-solveable problem.

The more you write, the better your critical thinking gets.

This is the gift your brain has given you. To think critically, from a perspective that is uniquely yours.

Writing is where this gift blossoms. When you write, you force your brain to take the messy thoughts, silly things that bounce and wobble all over, and make them orderly. Make them logical. Make them into something that other people can read, and understand, and learn from.

This is why writing matters, and it's why writing a thesis matters. You will do a lot, in your life. You will contribute to many people's lives, in many ways. Writing—a thesis, a novel, a self-help book, or a thoughtful email—is a way for you to have your unique voice, your unique perspective, be part of the on-going human conversation.

I hope you found something helpful in this book. I hope that, whatever comes next, you can look back on your thesis, or your dissertation, and be proud of what you accomplished.

More than anything, though, I hope that you come away from this book knowing that whatever grad school throws at you, you can handle it.

Because you can.

REFERENCES

Part I: Things I Actually Cited

Bland, H. W., Melton, B. F., Bigham, L. E., & Welle, P. D. (2014). Quantifying the impact of physical activity on stress tolerance in college students. *College Student Journal, 48*(4), 559-568.

Boss, A. D., & Sims, H. P. Jr. (2008). Everyone fails! Using emotion regulation and self-leadership for recovery. *Journal of Managerial Psychology, 23,* 135-150.

Briggs, J. B. (1991, May 10). I don't know how to write. *We Are The Weird.* Republished online as "Write everyday." Retrieved from https://joebobbriggs.com/the-last-drive-in-a-joe-bob-original-how-to-be-a-writer/?v=0a10a0b3e53b

Cabrera-Caban, E., Garden, R., White, A., & Reynoldson, K. (2016, April). Mindfulness-based interventions: A brief review of their application to graduate student strain. *The Industrial-Organizational Psychologist, 53*(4). Retrieved from https://archive.org/details/461_20231114/534/

Csikszentmihalyi, M. (2008). *Flow: The psychology of optimal experience*. New York, NY: Harper Collins.

Finn, E., (2017). Swearing: The good, the bad & the ugly. *ORTESOL Journal, 34,* 17-26. https://files.eric.ed.gov/fulltext/EJ1152392.pdf

Futch, W., Gordon, N. S., & Gerdes, A. C. (2025). Student wellness: Interest and program ideas & pilot of a student wellness program. *Journal of American College Health, 73*(1), 235–243. https://doi.org/10.1080/07448481.2023.2214241

Kanfer, R. & Ackerman, P. L. (1989). Motivation and cognitive abilities: an integrative/aptitude-treatment interaction approach to skill acquisition. *Journal of Applied Psychology, Monograph, 74,* 657-690.

Kruisselbrink Flatt, A. (2013). A suffering generation: Six factors contributing to the mental health crisis in North American higher education. *College Quarterly, 16*(1), n1.

Mueller, P. A., & Oppenheimer, D. M. (2014). The pen is mightier than the keyboard: Advantages of longhand over laptop note-taking. *Psychological Science, 25*(6), 1159–1168.

Pirsig, R. M. (2006). *Zen and the art of motorcycle maintenance: An inquiry into values.* New York, NY: HarperTouch.

Poeppelman, T., & Blacksmith, N. (2014, January). Personal branding via social media: Increasing SIOP visibility one member at a time. *The Industrial-Organizational Psychologist, 51*(3), 112-119. Available from https://archive.org/details/461_20231114/513/page/n1/mode/2up

Pollitt, E., & Mathews, R. (1998). Breakfast and cognition: An integrative summary. *American Journal of Clinical Nutrition, 67*(4), 804S–813S.

Scully, D., Kremer, J., Meade, M., Graham, R., & Dudgeon, K. (1998). Physical exercise and psychological well being: A critical review. *British Journal of Sports Medicine, 32,* 111-120. doi: 10.1136/bjsm.32.2.111

Srna, S., Schrift, R. Y., & Zauberman, G. (2018). The illusion of multitasking and its positive effect on performance. *Psychological Science, 29,* 1942-1955. https://doi.org/10.1177/0956797618801

Storm, B. C., Bjork, E. L., & Bjork, R. A. (2005). Social metacognitive judgments: The role of retrieval-induced forgetting in person memory and impressions. *Journal of Memory and Language, 52,* 535-550.

Taras, H. (2005). Nutrition and student performance at school. *Journal of School Health, 75*(6), 199–213.

Trockel, M. T., Barnes, M. D., & Egget, D. L. (2000). Health-related variables and academic performance among first-year college students: Implications for sleep and other behaviors. *Journal Of American College Health, 49*(3), 125-131.

Part Two: Things I didn't cite, but recommend for further reading

Bell, S. (2007). *The artful edit: On the practice of editing yourself.* New York: W.W. Norton & Company.

Goodson, P. (2013). *Becoming an academic writer: 50 exercises for paced, productive, and powerful writing.* Los Angeles: Sage.

King, S. (2010). *On writing: A memoir of the craft.* New York, NY: Scribner.

Lerner, B. (2010). *The forest for the trees (revised and updated): An editor's advice to writers.* New York, NY: The Berkley Publishing Group.

Sterner, T. M. (2012). *The practicing mind: Developing focus and discipline in your life — master any skill or challenge by learning to love the process.* Novato, CA: New World Library.

Strunk, W., & White, E. B. (1999). *The elements of style* (4th ed.). Boston: Allyn & Bacon.

Truss, L. (2006). *Eats, shoots & leaves: The zero tolerance approach to punctuation*. New York, NY: Gotham Books.

Turabian, K. L. (2018). *A manual for writers of research papers, theses, and dissertations: Chicago Style for students and researchers* (9th ed.). Chicago: The University of Chicago Press.

Zinsser, W. (2016). *On writing well: The classic guide to writing nonfiction (30 Anv Rep Edition)*. New York: Harper Perennial.

ACKNOWLEDGMENTS

For a book that feels so short (I say this in comparison to some of the fiction manuscripts I've written over the years), there are an awful lot of people I need to thank for supporting it, and me. Before I do so, let me make it clear that while many of them have contributed insights or observations that informed my writing, any errors are mine and mine alone. The same goes for anything dumb, or anything that you try that doesn't work. That's all on me.

I have to start by thanking the 200+ students who went through our I-O psychology Master's program before its closure. Getting to give writing-related feedback to all of you helped me understand the variety of ways students approach the writing process and allowed me to continually refine my mentorship. The conversations and email exchanges about writing formed the core of what I felt like I had to say, that made this book possible.

Then there were the 80-odd students whose theses I actually chaired. Working with every one of you was rewarding, because I got to watch you grow as writers through your hard work. And, again, I learned how to better guide students through the thesis process by working with you.

My colleagues at Xavier University's School of Psychology who read early drafts of this book and, in some cases, assigned pieces of it to their classes, were invaluable. I could just list everyone in the department, really, but I'd especially like to thank Drs. Dalia Diab, Cindy Dulaney, and Kathy Hart, who not only read and provided comments early on, but were instrumental (especially Kathy!) in encouraging me to take the sabbatical to finish and publish this.

Speaking of my sabbatical, my sincere thanks go to Xavier University and its Faculty Development Committee for granting me the time to focus on this book and get it ready to share with the world. Xavier has helped me understand the kind of educator I want to be, and has supported me throughout my career in becoming that educator.

When I talked about an alpha reader who sat with me on the floor and helped me re-organize index cards, that was Rachel Geil. Rachel was a phenomenal graduate assistant, a fantastic thesis advisee, and is now a wonderful professional. Her input and insights from a grad student's perspective, and her creative and thoughtful approach to helping me with my vision for this book, were critical.

My beta readers as I was pushing down the "home stretch" were fantastic. Huge thanks to Megan Church-Nally, Mike Horvath, Megan Leasher, and Erik Zito.

And I couldn't really do an acknowledgments section without recognizing the influence my family has had on me, both as a writer and as an educator. My mom has been and continues to be an enduring influence, and has been a source of support and encouragement my entire life. She has strength reserves that defy expectations! My brother Jeff and my sister Carol have brilliant academic brains, and I have to struggle sometimes to feel like I'm living up to the chronological accident of being the eldest sibling.

We lost my dad a year and a half before I published this book; he read an early draft, and I hope he's proud of what I've done. You saw how many times I mentioned his influence, but believe me when I say that I didn't mention it nearly as much as I could have.

Finally, when it comes to supporting me and my writing, there is no one who has done more than my wife. Thank you, Christy. "I love you" doesn't begin to cover it.

ABOUT THE AUTHOR

Morrie Mullins was surprised, when he asked the software to insert an "about the author" page, to learn that he is apparently "an emerging author of young adult romance." He'd been laboring under the illusion that he was a writer, educator, and editor, that he loves creating speculative fiction that mashes up fantasy and science fiction elements, that he's been an academic teaching in psychology programs for a quarter-century, and that although he's published his fair share of articles and book chapters, this is his first solo-published book. He maintains a modest presence on social media, and more information about his writing, thinking, and pseudo-random braining can be found at https://www.morriemullins.com. Assuming he can get it online and keep it online, of course!

He presently has no plans to write young adult romance, though. Just for the record.

www.ingramcontent.com/pod-product-compliance
Lightning Source LLC
Chambersburg PA
CBHW020418150626
46554CB00014B/1923